The Power of the Cross

The Power of the Cross

Alan Vincent

© Copyright 2017 - Alan Vincent

All rights reserved. This book is protected by the copyright laws of the United States of America. This book may not be copied or reprinted for commercial gain or profit. The use of short quotations or occasional page copying for personal or group study is permitted and encouraged. Permission will be granted upon request. Unless otherwise identified, Scripture quotations are taken from the New King James Version. Copyright © 1982 by Thomas Nelson, Inc. Used by permission. All rights reserved. Scripture quotations marked NIV are taken from The Holy Bible, New International Version, Copyright © 1973, 1978, 1984 by International Bible Society. Used by Permission. Emphasis within Scripture quotations is the author's own.

ISBN-13: 9781546663898
ISBN-10: 1546663894

Endorsements

The Power of the Cross unpacks what gives the Gospel power to transform. The apostle Paul said he determined to know *nothing* but Jesus Christ and Him crucified. That makes this important topic central to Christianity. Alan Vincent does a superb job of unpacking the truths of Scripture around this theme in a way that any reader will understand. The apostolic preaching of the Cross has been the force behind the spread of Christianity on the earth and must be renewed in our current time while many are turning to self-help themes. There is no transformation of our souls without the application of the Cross to our lives. This book will lead you to that power.
—Barry Wissler, President, HarvestNET International, Ephrata, PA

I first met Alan Vincent about twenty-five years ago as he and his wife, Eileen, were preaching in our city. I was helping to pastor a growing church that desired a fuller expression of Jesus and His Kingdom. As I listened to Alan speak, I thought, *Am I even reading the same Bible? Where did this man get this revelation from?* As the years passed, we were influenced more and more by both Alan's life and his message. The message of the Cross was a profound stepping-stone in our journey in the Lord. As Alan unfolded this deep and central message of the Bible, we began to see much more fully what Jesus meant when He cried, "It is finished!" Our lives have been forever altered. Within the pages of this book is one of the central keys to all that God has for us in His Son. Read with a continual open ear to heaven, and you will never be the same for you will be transformed by *The Power of the Cross!*
—Randy Boyd, Director, Prepare International, Lubbock, TX

When I read the first few pages...my spirit exploded in boldness and praise! We are in an hour of history that the clarion call of the Cross must be released by those whose private and public lives have been transformed by it. God has found a man—a son—in Alan Vincent to do just that. Alan has penned some of the most needed and necessary truths to communicate the all-inclusive victory of Jesus Christ. He makes it clear that man's cleverness and charisma will never be enough to deal with the core issue of our defiled independence and all its subsequent issues. It is the Cross and only the Cross that can fully restore sons to the Father to live in abiding dependence...which brings total defeat to the enemy. I highly recommend you read and fully embrace *The Power of the Cross* for you personally...and then pass it on for the true discipleship of generations to come.
  —Nancy McCready, Executive Pastor, Christian City Fellowship, Sealy, TX.

Alan Vincent's book *The Power of the Cross* is both profound and simplistically applicable at the same time. Alan unveils the truth of the centrality of the Cross with clear apostolic authority and grace. This book is refreshing and convicting in a day when so many have shunned biblical absolutes. Thank you, Alan, for writing this powerful, impacting book for our generation!
  —Larry Kreider, Director, DOVE International

Contents

Endorsements · v

Foreword · ix

Chapter 1 The Need to Preach the Cross! · · · · · · · · · · · · · · · · · 1

Chapter 2 The Cross Is the Center · 5

Chapter 3 The Power of the Cross to Reconcile Us to God · · · · · · · · 16

Chapter 4 The Power of the Cross to Deal with the
Old Man · 24

Chapter 5 A New Heredity in Christ · 34

Chapter 6 The Power of the Cross to Crucify the Flesh · · · · · · · · · · · 50

Chapter 7 The Power of the Cross to Overcome
the World · 65

Chapter 8 The Power of the Cross to Ratify the Covenant—Part 1 · · · · 89

Chapter 9 The Power of the Cross to Ratify the Covenant—Part 2 · · · 109

Chapter 10   The Power of the Cross to Heal and Deliver Us from
             All Pain and Sickness ·121

Chapter 11   The Power of the Cross to Overcome Poverty · · · · · · · · ·131

Chapter 12   My Prayer for You to Know the Power of
             the Cross ·143

             Appendix I ·145

Foreword

It has been my joy and my burden to see this book published. Alan's ministry has touched countless people in many nations. Thriving churches and whole networks have been established through the impartation received through his revelatory teaching.

Alan preached the message of the Cross. It was foundational in his thinking. The way in which he enlarged upon the total breadth and power of the death, burial, and resurrection of Christ transformed his hearers. Today, many are well-known names in the church as they have built so well upon the foundational teachings they received. Because of the lasting fruit from Alan's ministry and many requests, I am convinced that the revelation given to Alan Vincent during his years of ministry has to be produced in books. With Natalie Hardy, I carefully prepared this material for publication.

Another provocation to see this book published came recently through a prophetic word given to Alan.

> *In you there is a generational mantle, a mantle of richness, and it is not going to fall to the ground. It is a mantle for wisdom and revelation; it must be transferred. The deposit in you is a treasure trove, coming as a mantle from heaven that is old and speaks of heritage. This cache is full of heaven's wisdom and nuggets of richness.*

I trust as you read this book you will find that prophetic word true for you. May the anointing of the Lord rest upon each page and then become revelation and blessing to your spirit.

—Eileen Vincent

CHAPTER 1

THE NEED TO PREACH THE CROSS!

And I, brethren, when I came to you, did not come with excellence of speech or of wisdom declaring to you the testimony of God. For I determined not to know anything among you except Jesus Christ and Him crucified. (1 Cor. 2:1–2)

The apostle Paul, in his statement above, declares that there is nothing to know except Jesus Christ and Him crucified, that Jesus' sacrifice on the Cross is the pinnacle event in history. How did he come to this conclusion and why?

First, let me give you some background to this 1 Corinthians passage. It is in Acts 16:8–18:1 that we read how Paul first brought the Gospel into what is today known as Europe. He originally had a great burden to move into an area of the Middle East that was then called Asia, present-day Turkey. In particular, he had his eye on the key city of Ephesus, where the famous Temple devoted to the worship of Diana was located. However, the Spirit of God did not permit him to go into Asia at that time. Instead, Paul received a vision of a man from Macedonia calling him to go and help the people of Europe, the area we know as the Balkans. He was immediately obedient to that visionary call and sailed to the region of Macedonia instead.

Paul's first encounter in Europe was in the city of Philippi. He then traveled to Thessalonica, Berea, and, finally, the great city of Athens—the former capital of the mighty Greek Empire. Athens had been conquered by the Romans centuries before and was in Paul's day part of the Roman

Empire, but it still remained the great Greek cultural and philosophical center for decades to come.

When Paul arrived in Athens, he found the whole city filled with intellectually minded people who spent their days discussing the meaning of life and man's purpose on earth. Those discussions are the foundation of modern humanism. The teaching of those great Greek philosophers, like Aristotle and Plato, is still studied and taught in universities all over the Western world today. The Greeks deified man, and they were convinced that the perfect man would emerge by the evolutionary development of his intellect; when this process was complete, it would result in a perfect man living in a perfect world.

Paul arrived in Athens and found all of these educated and intelligent people worshipping hundreds of different gods. He saw temple after temple dedicated to every kind of god that the Athenians could possibly imagine. He was very vexed in his spirit. The people of Athens believed in the unrestricted worship of anything and anyone. These very educated people believed that there was good in every sincerely held belief or point of view. To them everything was permissible, and no one should be so narrow as to say there is only one god, only one way to that god, and only one way to worship him. The ultimate example of Athenian liberalism was a temple dedicated to the "unknown god." This temple was built just in case they had accidentally overlooked a god. This temple was intended to meet the needs of any worshipper who could not find what he was looking for in any of the other temples.

Paul himself was a brilliant intellectual and well educated in Greek philosophy. He decided to use his intellectual prowess to win over the people of Athens. Paul's sermon to these philosophers is recorded in Acts 17:18–34. He was preaching on a hill in the center of Athens called Areopagus, a hill dedicated to Ares, the Greek god of war. Paul brilliantly appealed to the Greek philosophers and even quoted their poets so as to make his message more culturally relevant and hopefully more acceptable to their Athenian mind. He decided to do this as a clever way of appealing to them, and he spoke to them of this "unknown" god in a way that he hoped they would find acceptable. His sermon was a masterpiece of brilliant intellectual reasoning.

At first, they listened attentively, but when he mentioned the name of Jesus and the fact that He had risen from the dead, many just laughed at him in scorn and moved off to listen to more interesting speakers. A few people were touched and saved, but there was no significant response, no miracles, and no revival. And unlike his preaching to the religious Jews in Philippi, Thessalonica, and Berea, there was no fierce opposition followed by a riot in response to his "radical" teachings. In those places, hostile mobs had threatened Paul's life, leading to him being physically assaulted, thrown into jail, and finally expelled from every city he had visited.

In Athens, nothing major happened either way, and no significant church was established at that time. As a result, Paul left Athens in deep disappointment to move on to the next city, Corinth. However, I have a feeling that something was happening inside Paul during his long walk from Athens to Corinth. He was disturbed and puzzled by his failure to make any significant impact in Athens. I can imagine him questioning himself, "Lord what went wrong in Athens? Why did I not see the power I normally see? Why was there no revival or at least a riot? Something went wrong there. Only a few people believed. We left a tiny little church with very few believers and Athens has remained unchanged. Why?" I can imagine God replying to him, "You didn't preach the Cross. You never mentioned it because you felt it would seem too foolish to these educated, intellectual people. I don't want you ever to be ashamed of the Cross of Jesus Christ, for it is the power of God unto salvation to everyone who believes."

Athens and Corinth were very different cities. While Athens was the intellectual center of the area, Corinth was the commercial and trade center for the whole region of Macedonia and Achaia. From Corinth, ships sailed to all of the major ports of the Mediterranean, even as far east as India. Many ships were coming and going all the time, which made Corinth a very rich, sophisticated, and cosmopolitan city. And it was also very immoral.

By the time he arrived in Corinth, Paul had made up his mind that he would never again make the mistake of not preaching the Cross. Once in Corinth, he records in his first letter to the Corinthian church, "I was determined to know nothing among you except Jesus Christ and Him crucified" (1 Cor. 2:2).

The preaching of the Cross was paramount in my own personal experience of salvation. As the Cross was explained to me, an intellectual and self-declared scientific atheist, I saw my need to believe in Jesus and to receive His gift of salvation. My full salvation testimony is in Appendix I.

The following chapters will unfold the beauty, power, and mystery of the Cross of Christ, His death, burial, and glorious resurrection. May you be drawn into the wonders of God's love as you meditate upon these great themes.

CHAPTER 2

THE CROSS IS THE CENTER

In Corinth, the apostle Paul declared that he had only one objective among them. "I was determined to know nothing among you but Jesus Christ and Him crucified" (1 Cor. 2:2). He remained in Corinth for two years, and a mighty church was raised. My appeal to you in this book is to get the Cross right back into the center of all of your dealings with God, with the Devil, with the world, and with your life. This teaching is like a clarion call from God's Holy Spirit to His people at this time. In all the teaching of the great truths of the Kingdom, we must not lose sight of the foundation, the centrality, and power of the Cross of Jesus Christ.

I am sometimes appalled that many Christians, particularly charismatic Christians, can be so experience-orientated that they are interested in nothing else. Frequently they have no depth of understanding and no solid biblical foundation beneath these sometimes wonderful experiences that they may have had. We must have solid biblical understanding of the Cross to be able to stand against all the deceiving ways of the Devil, experience continuous victory over sin, and so remain standing and victorious in the hour of trial. In so doing, we will be able to enter into all the rich treasure that has been made available to us, through the power of the Cross.

In 1 Corinthians, chapters 1 to 3, Paul deals with the importance of bringing the church back to the profound simplicity of the Cross of Jesus Christ. He warns believers to be careful that the wisdom of words does not prevent them from allowing the Cross to have its full, powerful impact in their lives when he says, "For Christ did not send me to baptize, but to preach the Gospel, not with the wisdom of words, lest the Cross of Christ should be made of no effect" (1 Cor. 1:17). Apply this personally in your life. The Cross is not something you leave behind once you are saved. The Cross is an eternal, permanent, mighty power that must increase and continue to work in your life.

It is easy to dilute the power of the Cross in the wisdom of words. For example, it is very common in much Christian counseling to dig through a person's history to discover where the painful wounds are in their subconscious for the purpose of bringing the individual to healing or maturity. But often we have become so clever in our humanistic and psychological methodology that we fail to recognize the power of the Cross and what Jesus did there to purchase our healing and maturity.

1 Corinthians 1:18 says, "For the message of the cross is foolishness to those who are perishing, but to us who are being saved it is the power of God." Notice this verse is in the present-continuous tense. There are three tenses used regarding our salvation in scripture. Firstly, scripture sometimes says, "We have been saved"; that is past tense. Secondly, it sometimes says, "We are being saved"; that is present tense. Thirdly, it also sometimes says, "We will be saved," which is future tense. This passage, in the present-continuous tense, means the Cross is continuously the power of God to those who are saved. What a glorious thought: the power of the Cross of Jesus Christ is available to every believer today and always.

The Cross is the solution to the long-standing problems you may be experiencing in your life. I preach the Cross with all my heart not just on Easter Sunday but all the time. The power of the Cross is to be permanently and constantly working in all our lives.

Paul divided the world essentially into two categories: those to whom the message of the Cross was foolishness and those to whom the message was the power of God unto salvation. Which is it in your life? What is the Cross doing in you? How is the power of the Cross working in you and through you? As you read the following pages, open your heart and let the Spirit of God teach you these things since He is the one who longs to reveal the full power of the Cross to every believer.

The Cross versus the Wisdom of the World

> *For it is written: "I will destroy the wisdom of the wise, and bring to nothing the understanding of the prudent." Where is the wise? Where is the scribe? Where is the disputer of this age? Has not God made foolish the wisdom of this world? For since, in the wisdom of God, the world through wisdom did not know God, it pleased God through the foolishness of the message preached to save those who believe. For Jews request a sign, and Greeks seek after wisdom; but we preach Christ crucified, to the Jews a stumbling block and to the Greeks foolishness, but to those who are called, both Jews and Greeks, Christ the power of God and the wisdom of God. Because the foolishness of God is wiser than men, and the weakness of God is stronger than men.* (1 Cor. 1:19–25)

Do you agree with this scripture? It is very important that you should. There are people who have seen all kinds of incredible miracles and are convinced of the power of God, yet their lives are still a mess in many respects because they have never let the Cross do its sanctifying work in them. Miracles are an attesting sign to the truth of the Gospel, but they are not the power of the Gospel. The Cross is the power of the Gospel. The Jews were looking for a sign and a miracle, and the Greeks were seeking for wisdom. However, the Greeks were looking for the wrong kind of wisdom. They sought the wisdom of this world, which could not really help them. It is the Cross that is the power of God unto salvation.

It is very important that we have signs and wonders to establish the power of the Gospel. However, signs and wonders do not change people's lives. Signs and wonders are often necessary to open a person to hear the Gospel. But it is the message of the Cross that actually transforms people. Miracles alone do not. Signs and wonders might touch their bodies physically, but it is the power of the Cross that transforms them permanently—body, soul, and spirit.

Two years before my conversion, I left my position as a research scientist at the Kodak Film Company in Harrow, England, and moved into the academic arena. I lectured full time in the College of Advanced Technology, and it was during that time I was saved. Once saved, all my plans changed and instead of going to America I returned to Kodak, England, but this time to a more senior position leading a scientific research team. I thought to myself, *Well, now that I am a Christian, I must somehow try to reach my colleagues for Christ.* At first, I tried to be intellectual about the Gospel, just like Paul had done in Athens, but like Paul, it did not work for me either.

I vividly remember one experience I had with a very senior member of our research staff. He was an internationally famous scientist, a leading expert in his field. One day he telephoned me and said, "Alan, come into my laboratory. I want to show you something. I have developed a new incredibly fine-grain emulsion." I went running into his laboratory, and he put a slide under the microscope and said to me, "Have a look, and you will see how beautifully fine this emulsion grain is." I looked down the microscope and focused it carefully. Do you know what I saw? I saw a microscopic picture of a blatantly nude woman. He thought it was a great joke to play on me.

I turned around to this man and said to him, "Sir! You have a great intellect, and in terms of scientific reputation, you are one of the world's greatest authorities on the theory of the photographic process. But on the inside, you are just a dirty old man and you need a Savior just like I did." I gave this man fifteen minutes of simple Gospel truth about Jesus and how He was crucified for sinners like him and me. He stood there with his mouth wide open, and I could feel the throbbing power of the Spirit as I preached the Cross to him. I thought to myself, *Forget about all this intellectualism. From now on, I will just preach the foolishness of the Cross! That's where the power is.*

Paul instructs believers in 1 Corinthians that the message of the Cross has to be articulated. It has to be preached and spoken out. I want to exhort you, wherever you go during your working week, be determined to know nothing among your colleagues except Jesus Christ and Him crucified and the power of God will be with you. I decided from that day forward that I was going to be boldly unashamed of the apparent foolishness of the Cross. So I became the active leader of an evangelistic organization within the factory of Kodak in Harrow, England, which in those days had about ten thousand employees. I would stand on a table in the worker's canteen during their lunch hour and preach for twenty minutes to them about the Lord Jesus and the Cross.

Just before I was converted, I had said to my wife, Eileen, that if I ever became a Christian I was going to be a *real* one. I was now having to prove that I meant what I said. Over the years, I have seen amazing miracles of healing and transformation of people's lives take place through the simple preaching of the Cross of Jesus Christ. Whether I am talking to a Hindu; a Muslim; a nominal Christian, or a sophisticated intellectual, agnostic, or atheist, I share the same message of the power of the Cross.

Truth and Absolutes

For I am not ashamed of the gospel of Christ, for it is the power of God to salvation for everyone who believes, for the Jew first and also for the Greek. (Rom. 1:16)

We enjoy in our Western society, particularly in America and Europe, a way of thinking that is peculiar to our culture, which is not found in other areas of the world. Western society is different. I would suggest this is a direct result of our Judeo-Christian heritage where there is an understanding of what truth is, of what is right and wrong. Unfortunately, as societies move away from its biblical roots this is being lost. I lived in Bombay, India, for thirteen years, and like most of Asia, India is not a Judeo-Christian society and therefore lacks understanding of the absolute truth.

This belief in absolute right and wrong is peculiar to societies that have to some extent come to know the true God and the power of the Cross. Even in the Western world, there was a difference in the definition of truth. While the Renaissance and its Greek-philosophical influence were "enlightening" the people of southern Europe, the northern European countries experienced the Reformation. This was a time when Christians returned to the scriptures accepting them as the absolute truth and the determinant of right and wrong. For example, Spain, Italy, and large parts of France have a very different idea of truth than those countries of Europe that were most affected by the Reformation. The Founding Fathers of North America were predominately from the Reformation nations and believed in absolute truth based on the Word of God. They were unlike those who experienced the Renaissance, who did not believe in absolute truth but were instead dictated to by the wisdom of the wise.

In the beginning chapters of Paul's first letter to the Corinthians, he sets out to clearly demonstrate this wisdom of the "wise" is of no value because it cannot discern truth. The only real truth is in God Himself.

For you see that if something is right in God's eyes, then its opposite cannot also be right at the same time or indeed have any truth in it at all. If Jesus is the true Savior of the world, then there is no other Name under heaven by which anyone can be saved. That is a plain and simple statement of scripture. There is nothing in Hinduism, Islam, any other religion, or any philosophy that has any saving power. These religious systems can only take a person away from the truth. They cannot in any way be the truth or lead anyone to the truth. Jesus said, "I am the way, I am the truth and I am the life. No man can come to the Father except by Me" (John 14:6). The Bible also says, "for there is no other name under heaven given among men by which we must be saved" (Acts 4:12). However, today's educational institutions require that their students consider all religions to be true.

If you go through the scriptures, you will find that they are full of black-and-white statements, what I would call absolutes. The Cross was and is one of those absolutes. It deals radically, permanently, and finally with life's most important issues, gives eternal life, speaks truth, and settles other eternal issues. If you do not think straight, in terms of absolutes, like God does, then you cannot experience the power of the Cross. You must let God bring you to a place where He metamorphoses your mind so that you begin to think like God.

Thesis–Antithesis Thinking versus Synthetic Thinking

There is a definite way that God thinks. He thinks in terms of absolute right and wrong. His way of thinking has a philosophical name which is called "thesis–antithesis" thinking. Its basic premise is that there is right and there is wrong in absolute terms. If something is true, then anything that is not of that truth and contradicts that truth cannot have any truth in it at all and therefore is false. That is the Judeo-Christian way of thinking.

Most of the world does not even know or believe in absolute truth. When Pilate said, "What is truth" (John 18:38), he was not being particularly cynical. He was speaking from his own cultural experience. His Greco-Roman culture did not know any real truth because everything was relative and everybody played the game of situational ethics. They chose to believe, speak, and do whatever seemed to be in their best interests at any given time and to do whatever was perceived to be to their best advantage regardless of what the facts were in absolute terms.

At the turn of the nineteenth century, our educational institutions, first in Europe and then in the United States, experienced a dramatic change in their way of thinking. These institutions were invaded with a new, powerful intellectual force that was seeking to cause change in all our educational institutions and was determined to persuade everyone to accept a new, more broad-minded way of thinking—called "synthetic thinking."

Synthetic thinking teaches that any sincerely held belief must have some value and be accepted as an equally valid point of view. It attempts to find the best of what is possibly the truth in a compromised patch-up of various sincerely held beliefs. The "synthetic thinker" reasons that we cannot reject anything as being absolutely wrong because that is not a proper intellectual approach. We must be open-minded and be open to reason. We must recognize that there is some value in every sincerely held belief. Therefore, to them there must be some truth in Hinduism, in Islam, in Christianity, and especially in ancient Greek philosophy. Synthetic thinkers believe we must consider all of these as relative truths and the different opinions that they represent, and then gradually we will evolve toward "real" truth that we will find somewhere in a synthesized blend of all these different opinions.

That of course is a fallacy, but it is gripping the minds of most of the intellectual world today. Synthetic thinking goes right back to ancient Greek philosophy, the same thing Paul encountered in Athens. We have come full circle after two thousand years. The full return to this was accomplished through the birth of what was called the "Age of Reason," which began toward the end of the nineteenth century and gained momentum in the early part of the twentieth century.

Mainly German philosophers and some British thinkers like Julius Huxley were largely responsible for this influence. One of the reasons

Nazism found such fertile soil in Germany in the 1930s was due to this change in thinking. They abandoned their "thesis–antithesis" thinking and embraced the error of "synthetic thinking." Once you abandon your belief in an absolute right or wrong and in eternal truth, you become lost in a sea of "anything goes and everything is acceptable."

Each one of us has been bombarded by synthetic thinking throughout most of our education. It is the deliberate policy of almost every Western educational institution to break any perceived narrowness of thought or inherited "bigotry" so as to make us abandon absolutes. You are not allowed to have definite predetermined morals or beliefs based on biblical truth. If you do, then you are regarded as having a closed mind. These institutions consider it their responsibility to break open the minds of every student so that he or she will abandon moral absolutes and instead consider and accept many different points of view.

In synthetic thinking, you are taught to take the broadest possible scope of information without drawing definite conclusions. It is a way of thinking that does not deny anything but embraces everything. The result is definite immoral opinions or a variety of strong views about almost everything. Everything becomes relative because absolute biblical truth is abandoned.

Synthetic thinking has had the effect of producing national and political leaders with no deep moral convictions about anything. These leaders do not have any fear of the one true God. Almost no one in these circles has anything they truly, deeply believe in anymore. As a result, society has become bereft of real moral leadership. There are very few outstanding leaders with a passion for righteousness and truth—leaders who can inspire people to be willing to live or die for absolute truth. Can you see how this malaise has permeated all of our society? It all goes back to the "new" way we have been taught to think—that is, synthetic thinking.

Renew Your Mind

Ever since I was saved and filled with God's Holy Spirit, I have been through a total transformation in the way that I think. I think in a different way altogether now. Now my life is governed by the absolute Truth of God's Word revealed by His Holy Spirit. It is the criterion by which everything else must be judged and measured.

While now I have come to a place where I believe with all my being in the infallibility of God's Word, for several years, I am ashamed to say, I threw away the New Testament my grandmother would give me every Christmas. I know now if it says it in the Bible, then that is good enough for me, and it settles the issue of right and wrong. What is more, God Himself spoke through those who wrote the scriptures and caused them to write His Word exactly the way He meant it. I remember being taught this principle in my early days as a new believer. "God has said it and that settles it" has been the foundation of my thinking ever since.

If this renewing of your mind has not already taken place, then I want you to cry out to God that it happens to you right away. We are repeatedly exhorted to renew our minds so we can actually begin to think like God. Paul said, "And do not be conformed to this world, but be transformed by the renewing [literally metamorphosisf your mind that you may prove what is the good, acceptable and perfect will of God" (Rom. 12:2).

I want to ask some of you, particularly those who have been through the higher forms of education, this question, "Has your mind been renewed? Do you now think like God?" God has said in Isaiah 55:8–9,

For My thoughts are not your thoughts, nor are your ways My ways, says the Lord. For as the heavens are higher than the earth, so are My ways higher than your ways, and My thoughts than your thoughts.

The Cross cannot do its work in you until you are prepared and able to think like God. This means accepting the black-and-white statements of scripture as nonnegotiable truths. They have all the authority of the Eternal God behind them. This is very important. The wisdom that is of this world cannot change you; only the Cross can do this miraculous work in your life. You have to think like God in order to receive the wisdom that comes down from above.

For example, Paul says in 1 Corinthians 1:23, "We preach Christ crucified: a stumbling block to Jews and foolishness to Gentiles." Christ crucified was a stumbling block to the Jews because it meant that all their religious activity was of no value whatsoever. Some of you may say, "Do you mean to say that if a person has done forty years of faithful devotion to some kind of religious activity that it is worthless?" That is exactly what I'm saying, because the Bible clearly says it.

If you are a Hindu or a Muslim, it is equally true. If you are a Christian, who has not put your trust in the Cross but only in the traditions and activities of your Christian church denomination, then it is also true for you. We are told in Isaiah 64:6 that all our righteousness (meaning the good things we try to do to earn merit with God) is as filthy rags in His eyes. This is because of the wrong motives with which we have done them. We may have been unconsciously believing, "I'm doing these things to earn merit and favor with God. Look what a good Christian I am." Once you say or think that kind of thing, all those righteous acts become filthy rags in the eyes of God. They are polluted with self-esteem and with the seeking of merit before God and men. That is the truth. Until we start to think right, we cannot receive the power of the Cross.

Let's consider the many great dimensions of the Cross that we will be looking at as we proceed through this book. They are as follows:

The power of the Cross to reconcile us to God
The power of the Cross to deal with the old man
The power of the Cross to deal with the flesh
The power of the Cross to deal with the world
The power of the Cross to ratify the covenant
The power of the Cross to deal with all sicknesses
The power of the Cross to deliver me from poverty and prosper me

Before we continue, let us pray for the Lord to renew our minds:

Dear God, I know the Cross is so important. Although we can never fully understand this great mystery, I want the power of the Cross to work in my life. Lord, I want to have my mind renewed to think like You (Rom. 12:2) and become an absolute, eternal, right and wrong thinker. Deliver me from any damage to my thinking that has come through the education I have received. Bring me back to the simplicity and the profundity of thinking like You.

Lord, I believe there are absolutes. The things that you have said in Your Word are truths that are nonnegotiable. They are absolutely true and right. All the opposites of those things are entirely wrong. There is no good in them at all. There is no middle ground of compromise. Right at the center of Your truth is the Cross of Jesus Christ. Open my eyes to the Cross; let the power of it begin to throb in a new way in my life. Amen.

CHAPTER 3

THE POWER OF THE CROSS TO RECONCILE US TO GOD

In the beginning, God created man in His own image and likeness. He breathed the breath of life into him. He walked with him in fellowship in the garden. Man was God's supreme creation, into whom God deposited the ability to exercise His rule upon the earth. They had mutual love and fellowship with one another. Then came sin.

Adam stepped out of this glorious relationship *with* God into independence *from* God. He made his own decision to eat that which had been forbidden and in so doing became separated from the life of God, which produced spiritual death. His spiritual death was the result of his sin. And, as the apostle Paul writes in Romans 5:12, "through one man sin entered the world, and death through sin...thus death spread to all men because all sinned." Adam's sin passed on to all men.

In the very beginning, God had a plan to rescue His creation from sin and reconcile them to Himself. His plan was Jesus, His only Son, who was crucified, before the foundation of the earth.

Who can ever plumb the deep meaning of the Cross? Its reach is into all mankind, reconciling them to God. When Jesus died on the Cross, He made a way for God to forgive us and take away our sin. Jesus died on the Cross to satisfy God's wrath for our sin. Jesus died on the Cross and canceled the certificate of debt against us. Because of the Cross, there is now no condemnation.

Jesus Died So God Could Forgive Us

We are all born with a sinful nature. Our Holy God cannot abide the presence of sin. We cannot be in relationship with Him. Jesus's first work on the Cross was dying for us to enable God to forgive us and take away all our sin. His death paid the legal penalty for sin and removed all legal claims of Satan upon our lives.

The Certificate of Debt Against Us

In Paul's letter to the Colossians, he describes the state of man, "And you, being dead in your trespasses and the uncircumcision of your flesh" (Col. 2:13). That was our condition—dead in our sin. All that lay before us was the torment of hell. Once we have left this life, we would go for all eternity into the fullness of hell. There was no way out. There was no escape. As we begin to grasp what God did in Christ at the Cross, we realize that there is no other message and no other solution to man's completely helpless condition except the Cross! This is what fuels my passion for evangelism. Someone may be nice or nasty by average worldly standards, but when measured by God's standards, they are already dead in their sin and there is no hope for them except in the Cross.

In God's sight, there is an enormous mountain of debt existing against each one of us. We can try to take that debt upon ourselves and in some futile way try to pay for it by doing good works, but it's impossible for each one of us to do so. Even if we were able to live up to the impossible standard of living perfectly, without sin for the rest of our lives, it still would not deal with our sinful past. All that it would achieve would be to stop adding to our list of previous sins; even living a perfect life from here on out would not remove the debt from our past. In practice, each one of us would actually be adding to the debt of sin against us every day that we lived, if it were not for that glorious Cross. No one except Jesus has ever lived a perfect life. All we can do is to joyfully and thankfully let Him take all our sins—past, present, and future—and pay the full debt on our behalf.

The Bible says this is what Jesus did:

Having wiped out the handwriting of requirements (the certificate of debt) that was against us, which was contrary to us. And He has taken it out of the way, having nailed it to the cross. (Col. 2:14)

Jesus cried out on the Cross, "It is finished!" The Greek verb *teleos* means to completely finish something, to fully pay a debt, or complete a transaction. This word was particularly used in the realm of accounting and means "there is nothing left to pay." For example, imagine that you had a large debt with a moneylender. If someone else then came and paid the whole debt on your behalf so that you owed nothing anymore, then, as the whole debt was being fully paid, they would write across each canceled bill of debt this same word—*teleos*! "It is finished! Nothing to pay!" The debt has completely gone.

The Greek manuscript also tells us that when Jesus cried out on the Cross, it was not a cry of pain but a cry of victorious triumph, just like the cry that a gladiator makes as he executes the killing thrust in a battle. He makes that final thrust in full confidence that he now has the victory and it's all over! That was the cry of Jesus upon the Cross, "It's finished! *Teleos!* Nothing to pay!" He took the handwriting of all the debts that were against us and nailed them to the Cross, completely canceling them out. Hallelujah!

We must walk in the balance of the truth. The Bible says in John 3:16, "God so loved the world that He gave His only begotten son" to die on the Cross for us. He died for the whole world, yet at the same time, we rejoice that He was willing to die just for me.

The Cross and the Wrath of God

Sin produces an outraged indignation that goes on and on called the wrath of God. It is not just temporary anger, but it is an eternal attitude.

If you were to sin now and then stop, God would still be as much offended by that past sin two or ten thousand years from now as He is today. Try to grasp these things. There is an eternal offence created in God's heart whenever we sin. God has no choice in this matter but to feel wrath because it is His very nature. The Cross was the place where the vilest of criminals were executed. Jesus had to die the death of a vile criminal because that is who you and I are in God's sight until cleansed from our sin. There was no way out of that. It had to be a vile, cruel, and brutal execution reserved for the worst kind of criminal. This fully shows us what God thinks about sin and how God is offended by it.

We must walk in the balance of the truth. The Bible says in John 3:16, "God so loved the world that He gave His only begotten Son" to die on the Cross for us. Yet at the same time we must realize it was absolutely necessary for Jesus to die in that terrible cruel way upon the Cross. It was not enough for Him to just die. It was not simply the death of Christ, but it was the death of Christ upon the Cross that released great power. We have to recognize the fact that our God is a God who exhibits wrath as well as love and mercy.

The wrath of God is a clear biblical teaching. It is not simply anger; it is much deeper. God's wrath flows out from His outraged offended righteousness. We must grasp this fact about God. Every act of sin produces this reaction in God. His righteousness is offended and outraged that His creation should sin against His will and against His laws. There is much teaching and preaching that denies the reality of this wrath, but it is clear from many scriptures that this is part of the true nature of God.

God is also a God of great compassion and of great love. He loves to heal our hurts and be reconciled to lost men and women. But that reconciliation must be preceded by genuine repentance from our rebellious sinfulness and independence. His wrath must be satisfied and we must turn from our independence to joyful submission to His rule and Lordship over our lives. Unfortunately, many Christian leaders and their people have so focused on God's unconditional love and mercy that they have lost the wrath dimension of our God completely.

Let me try to give you a simple illustration. Suppose a man had a little boy, and this father said to his little boy, "Son, we are going to church in an hour or two. You are all dressed up in your nice, clean Sunday clothes. Therefore, stay in the house. I don't want you to go anywhere before we leave for church." But the little boy disobeys his father and runs out of the house and meets some of his friends, and he goes into the neighbor's barn to play with them. While playing, he falls from the hayloft onto the floor below; he is injured and his clothes are now in a filthy dirty mess.

They bring this pathetic little child back home, and there is a problem. He is dirty; he is injured and in pain; and he has also blatantly disobeyed his father. It would not be enough for the father to just treat his wounds, wash his clothes, and comfort him to make him feel better. This is as far as some people go in preaching the Gospel. Their only message is that "Jesus loves you and He longs to heal you, clean you up and make you feel better."

Going back to our story, the father can put clean clothes on his wounded son, but that has not dealt with the "heart issue," the rebellion that caused the boy to blatantly disobey his father. The father must go further in dealing with his son. Of course, when Dad picks up his little boy, there is compassion and love in his heart, but he still has to deal with the disobedience. It is not enough to get his son clean clothes. He must deal with his son's rebellion. He must bring him to repentance and, if he truly loves his son, also punish him appropriately, even though it hurts both of them to do so.

In the Cross, we see the wrath of God against sin. It was not possible for Jesus to die in bed or be pushed over the cliff by those who hated him in Nazareth. It was not possible for Him to die in any other way than on the Cross because God had to pour out His wrath upon His Son. This was necessary so that all sin could be properly paid for and fully atoned for and then put away. There were no shortcuts to this. I want you to ask God to show you His hatred of sin. If we grasp this fact, it is going to change a lot of us and prevent a lot of us from sinning as quickly and as easily as we tend to do.

I am amazed how quickly some people, for instance, can fall back into immorality and immediately say, "Oh, the Lord will forgive me." Don't they understand what they have done? If there is true repentance, then it's true that the Lord will forgive even that sin. However, is there no horror in their heart for their sin and the way they have so displeased God? Can't we see what sinning does and how it offends God so much, that His wrath had to be poured out upon His beloved Son Jesus, as the only way by which He could freely forgive us?

Once we have grasped this truth, it has two effects upon us. First, we come to hate sin the way God hates it. Second, in a new way we come to Him in amazement and adoring thankfulness that Jesus was willing to take God's full wrath against sin upon Himself in our place. Jesus, instead of me and you, became the focus of the wrath of God against our sin. In the Cross, both the Father and the Son lovingly and joyfully cooperated together to allow for the restoration of our relationship with God.

These things are not said very much today, and yet until we grasp these truths, we cannot fully experience the power of the Cross. I stand in amazement that God should have set His love upon me. Just to be allowed to clean the floor in the furthest corner of heaven is so much more than I deserve, and it would be more than enough for me. God does not owe me anything. He does not owe you anything. If He blesses you or me, then it is because of His undeserved amazing grace. We have not earned anything, nor do we deserve a single thing.

Jesus, Our Propitiation

There is an old-fashioned English word, which is missing in some of our modern English translations. It is the word "propitiation" (Greek: *hilasmos*). It is used in the King James Bible and in the New King James Bible. For example, in 1 John 2:2, where the apostle John writes, "And He is the propitiation for our sins: and not for ours only, but also for the sins of the whole world." This word means to "fully pay for" or "to satisfy the wrath of an offended person." Modern translations tend not to use the old English word "propitiation," preferring the word "expiate."

Imagine that you were a businessperson and you called in an accountant to come and do an audit of your company. When he arrived, he found pages of unpaid debts on your books. He would not say, "Let's just tear out these pages of the past, throw them away, turn over to a new clean page, and pretend you don't owe anything. The business is in good shape." That would not be good enough for you, and it is not good enough for God either. He says, "I can't just forgive and forget your sin because My nature cannot simply ignore sin. I am a righteous God, a just Judge, and sin must be paid for."

So it was God's will that Jesus went to the Cross and was treated the way He was treated. He was not a victim of circumstances. It was the deliberate plan of God that He would be betrayed, humiliated, stripped naked, punched in the face, beaten with a Roman whip, and finally nailed to hang on a Cross. He was pulled down into the depths of Hades for the period of His suffering in order that sin could be fully paid for and the wrath of God be fully satisfied. It was all the deliberate, necessary plan of God. Remember the words of Isaiah, "Yet it pleased the LORD to bruise him. He has put Him to grief. When you made His soul an offering for sin" (Isa. 53:10).

When I began to grasp these things, tears poured down my cheeks. I sat in my study, thinking, *I just don't understand why You are so good to me. It is so undeserved. It is so unmerited.* But because I began to see and understand these things, I came to love my Savior much more deeply. I will do anything for Him. Nothing I do can possibly compare to what He has already done for me. So there is love, there is adoration, and there is gratitude and thankfulness. We cannot forget this dimension of the Cross—through the suffering of Jesus, God has totally satisfied His justice, His righteousness, and His wrath.

It has also made me really hate the sin that was in me, which required Jesus to suffer such punishment. Now I want no part of sin anymore. As I have already said, the sin is so completely paid for that the Devil's mouth is forever sealed; he cannot say anything against me now. He no longer has any claim over you or me because of what Jesus did! Remember, as He died, Jesus cried, "*Teleos!* It is finished." There is nothing to pay. I am totally forgiven and reconciled to God.

When the Devil comes against me, I will not receive his lies because there is no truth in them. He cannot accuse me of anything in my past life because I can confidently say to him, "Don't you know about the Cross? Stop accusing me with all those things that I did. All my debt has been paid! It has gone. I owe you nothing. Be gone in Jesus's Name."

The Cross and Condemnation

The Cross has dealt with every avenue of the Devil's accusation because of our sin. However, I find many Christians living in condemnation because they do not know this truth. Jesus said, "You shall know the truth and the truth will make you free" (John 8:32). Colossians 2:15 also explains that Jesus totally triumphed over the principalities and powers of Satan: "having disarmed them, He made a public spectacle of them, triumphing over them in it." When the Devil comes with his accusations and condemnation, you can now confidently declare because of the Cross the Devil now has no power or claim over me. The Devil has no more power over you than he has over Jesus.

Do you believe that? I have endeavored to live this way for many years now. When I began to see these things, my excitement went through the roof! If you do not grasp the wrath factor of the Cross, then you cannot grasp the full liberating factor of the Cross either. Once you see how totally and completely the Cross has paid for all your sin—past, present, and future—you are free from all accusation and any claim of the Devil upon your life. You are absolutely free. Hallelujah! Praise the Lord! As a result, you are absolutely filled with love and gratitude toward the One who did all this for you while you were still His enemy. In the wonderful words of Charles Wesley, "Amazing love. How can it be that You my God should die for me?"

Now I want to summarize what we have learned so far. The first work of Jesus on the Cross was to die for me in order to forgive and take away my sin completely. He paid for my sin and gave me new life.

Jesus also fully satisfied the wrath of God against sin and has made full propitiation for the outraged, righteous wrath of God against me, allowing me to be fully reconciled to God. Because of this, I may know Him as my Friend and as my loving Father just as Jesus does. Jesus also fully paid the full legal penalty for all my sin and has already removed all legal claims of Satan upon my life. It is finished! There is nothing left to pay!

Pray these precious truths into your heart.

Heavenly Father, as we contemplate what you have done for us through the perfect death of Jesus upon the Cross, we are left in wonder and deep gratitude. Father, nothing was overlooked as You orchestrated every detail of the betrayal of Jesus, the brutality by His captors, and His cruel death on the Cross. Through the sacrifice of your perfect Son for our sin and His outpoured blood, You reconciled us to Yourself, even though we were Your enemies and dead in our sins. You made a way where there was no way. Through the death of Jesus the Christ, You are now able, as the righteous judge, to fully forgive us as your justice is satisfied.

Thank You, Lord, for your magnificent love given to us in salvation.

CHAPTER 4

THE POWER OF THE CROSS TO DEAL WITH THE OLD MAN

> *What shall we say then? Shall we continue in sin that grace may abound? Certainly not! How shall we who died to sin live any longer in it? Or do you not know that as many of us as were baptized into Christ Jesus were baptized into His death? Therefore we were buried with Him through baptism into death, that just as Christ was raised from the dead by the glory of the Father, even so we also should walk in newness of life. For if we have been united together in the likeness of His death, certainly we also shall be in the likeness of His resurrection, knowing this, that our old man was crucified with Him, that the body of sin might be done away with, that we should no longer be slaves of sin. For he who has died has been freed from sin. Now if we died with Christ, we believe that we shall also live with Him, knowing that Christ, having been raised from the dead, dies no more. Death no longer has dominion over Him. For the death that He died, He died to sin once for all; but the life that He lives, He lives to God. Likewise you also, reckon yourselves to be dead indeed to sin, but alive to God in Christ Jesus our Lord. (Rom. 6:1–11)*

As we continue to explore the power of the Cross, recalling Paul's words and how he is determined to know nothing except Jesus and Him crucified, I will continue to the second great truth of the Cross, the power of the Cross to deal with the Old Man. The old man is translated as the "old self" in most newer Bible translations. By the time we get to the end of this chapter, I trust you will be rejoicing as you will understand the power of the Cross to deal with the old man.

The Death of the Old Man

To understand this truth, we will start with Paul's question to the Romans, found in Romans 6:1, "What shall we say then? Shall we continue in sin that grace may abound?" Paul is asking this question because he knows it is in the minds of many of the people who will read his letter. So he is addressing their thinking that perhaps the Gospel of Christ allows them to keep on sinning and asking for forgiveness as often as necessary. Paul answers this question with a vehement "Certainly not!" (Rom. 6:2). Literally, in Greek, Paul is saying, "Perish the thought!" or "Away with such an idea!"

Unfortunately, today, many Christians don't understand this. Instead, each Sunday they attend Church, praying for God to forgive them for the sins of the past week only to continue in sin for yet another week. But, through the power of the Cross, we have victory over this cycle.

To appreciate what Jesus did for us when He dealt with the old man, there are three points in Romans 6:1–11 that are absolute facts, which we must believe. The first one in verse 3 is, as believers, we are baptized into Christ's death. The second point, from verse 6, is "our old man was crucified with Him, that the body of sin might be done away with, that we should no longer be slaves of sin." And finally, in verse 9, "knowing that Christ, having been raised from the dead, dies no more. Death no longer has dominion over Him." Once we really know these three absolute truths, then we can reckon with absolute certainty on the fact that all three of them are working victoriously in our lives to gain victory over the old man. We can rejoice as verse 11 confirms that we are dead indeed to sin and alive in Christ!

If you have ever had any dealings with business accountants, then you know they are not "let's pretend people." I am sure you agree. If the IRS (Internal Revenue Service) arrives to examine your business accounts, they will only deal with the facts as written in the accounts and not with someone's optimistic imaginations. The word "reckon" that is used in Romans 6:11 is actually a word that was used in financial accounting in biblical days. Literally, the Greek verb "reckon" reflects the certainty of something you can count on. If an optimistic business owner were to say to his accountant, "I'm just going to believe we made over one hundred thousand dollars profit last year," then the accountant would respond, "Well, show me the proof." You cannot live in pretense when dealing with financial records. The accountant would insist, "I want to see the facts. Let me see what is actually written in your accounts. When I have seen the facts, then I can reckon what is the true profit of your company."

That is exactly what this word "reckon" means in Romans 6:11. When you have come to know certain facts written in the Word of God, then you can reckon on the certainty of those facts. You can reckon on those facts, in the same way that an accountant stands on the solid ground of proven financial facts. When he is convinced that the numbers in your accounts are absolutely real and true, then he can come to certain financial conclusions about the business. If the business is in the red, then an accountant will never say, "The business is actually in the red, and you are in real trouble, but let us all praise God 'by faith' and 'believe' that you are all living in financial success." To an accountant that is totally unreal. He says, "No, the facts don't tell me that. The facts say you are in serious financial trouble."

There is a false kind of the so-called faith practiced by some, which is like a game of "let's pretend" and imagination. But this is not faith at all. True faith is founded on solid facts that are written in the Word of God. These facts may violate our human logic or be contrary to our visible circumstances, but as far as God is concerned, they are absolutely true foundational facts. If God clearly says something, He means it and it is true.

In like manner, when God says something in a certain way He means it exactly the way that He has said it. If He uses the past tense, He means it is in the past. If He uses the future tense, He means it is in the future. If He uses the present tense, He means it is presently happening. That is so simple. And yet many Christians stumble over what God says and particularly the way He says it. They qualify the Word of God to fit their own prejudices or experiences rather than letting the Word of God speak for itself exactly as it is written.

For example, 2 Corinthians 5:17 says, "Therefore, if anyone is in Christ, he is [*already*] a new creation; old things have [*already*] passed away; behold, all things have [*already*] become new" The new has already come; the old has already passed away, and all is of God. These are all accomplished facts as far as the tenses are concerned.

Yet I hear some people pray as if they are going to be made into a new creature sometime in the future. The Bible doesn't say that. It says we are already a completely new creation. All the old has already passed. It is an accomplished fact. The new has already come—an accomplished fact. It is all of God, an accomplished fact. You may say, "Well, I don't understand that, and it doesn't feel like it." God doesn't ask you to understand it. He simply says, "Believe it!"

You see, the only way to think righteously is to think God's way; remember thesis–antithesis thinking. Whether you understand God's Word or not, get hold of it first of all in your spirit. Afterward, when you start to experience the truth of what you have already decided to believe, through faith, then your quickened spirit can begin to explain to your intellect what has already happened. Have you got it? If you wait to understand all that God has for you before you decide to believe it, then you will miss ninety-five percent of what God wants to give you.

It is a fact that you can get into a car and drive it without any need to understand how it works. Most people don't say, "I won't drive this car until I can understand how the electronic ignition works." If we said that, most of us would have to walk everywhere. So why can't we do the same thing in the spirit with God's written Word of truth? Why can't we just trust a perfect manufacturer, such as the Lord God Almighty, who knows how we are made? Let's just say, "I believe what God said, and I don't need to understand it intellectually before I decide to believe it."

In the Bible, God says what is true and what is not true. My response is to always say the same thing as God. You may think, *That's violating my intellect*. But it is not; it is bringing your intellect out of thinking in a wrong, worldly way into thinking like God.

The Law of Heredity
In this section, I will be making certain statements that are irrefutably biblical. However, they may not immediately make any sense to your natural mind, but do not worry about that. Just decide to believe them anyway.

Remember, we are not saved by knowledge but by faith, and this is how I continued to grow in grace as these truths were revealed to me by the Holy Spirit. Faith is the only way that you can be saved and appropriate these life-transforming truths.

First, let me introduce what I call the law of heredity. It is an oft-reported spiritual law in scripture. A good example of this is found in Hebrews 7:1–10:

> For this Melchizedek, king of Salem, priest of the Most High God, who met Abraham returning from the slaughter of the kings and blessed him, to whom also Abraham gave a tenth part of all, first being translated "king of righteousness," and then also king of Salem, meaning "king of peace," without father, without mother, without genealogy, having neither beginning of days nor end of life, but made like the Son of God, remains a priest continually.
>
> Now consider how great this man was, to whom even the patriarch Abraham gave a tenth of the spoils. And indeed those who are of the sons of Levi, who receive the priesthood, have a commandment to receive tithes from the people according to the law, that is, from their brethren, though they have come from the loins of Abraham; but he whose genealogy is not derived from them received tithes from Abraham and blessed him who had the promises. Now beyond all contradiction the lesser is blessed by the better. Here mortal men receive tithes, but there he receives them, of whom it is witnessed that he lives. Even Levi, who receives tithes, paid tithes through Abraham, so to speak, for he was still in the loins of his father when Melchizedek met him.

The law of heredity is illustrated in the example of Abraham and Levi in the above passage. The purpose of this passage is to prove that Melchizedek is a superior High Priest to Levi and he is the mediator of the new and better covenant.

If you are not already familiar with the story of how Abraham met Melchizedek, it is found in Genesis chapter 14. In our passage from Hebrews, the writer uses the story of Melchizedek to prove the biblical truth that I call the law of heredity; it is also a great example of how biblical logic works, something we need to understand. We are told in Hebrews 7 that when Melchizedek met Abraham certain things occurred between them that prove Melchizedek is clearly superior to Abraham.

Specifically, when Abraham met Melchizedek, Abraham offered tithes to Melchizedek and Melchizedek then blessed Abraham. The writer then asks the question: Which one is the greater, the one who blesses or the one who receives the blessing? Obviously, the answer is the one who gives the blessing. Therefore, we must conclude that Melchizedek is greater than Abraham. In the same way, the writer asks: Who is greater, the one who gives tithes or the one who receives tithes? Obviously, the one who receives tithes is greater. Melchizedek is again proved greater because he received tithes from Abraham. By these two proofs, the writer confirms that Melchizedek is greater than Abraham. As a result, we now have the great patriarch Abraham proven to be inferior to this Melchizedek.

In the next step of biblical logic, the writer states that at the time that Abraham offered tithes to Melchizedek, Levi, his great-grandson, was in the loins of Abraham. Neither Abraham's only son, Isaac, nor Isaac's son, Jacob, had been born. There were three unborn generations between Abraham and his great-grandson Levi.

Levi was inside Abraham's loins and, although unborn, he was involved with Abraham in his acts of submission to Melchizedek, actually participating with Abraham in those acts of submission. As Abraham offered tithes to Melchizedek, so did Levi. As Abraham had the blessing bestowed upon him, so did Levi. Through his hereditary line, Levi was in Abraham, giving the tithe, receiving the blessing, and submitting to the authority of Melchizedek.

Through this perfect biblical logic, the writer of Hebrews proves that Levi, like Abraham, is inferior to Melchizedek. Therefore, the priesthood of Levi must also be regarded as inferior to the priesthood of Melchizedek. Levi was in the loins of Abraham participating in his act of submission by paying tithes and in his act of receiving a blessing from the superior Melchizedek. As a result, in the New Covenant the priesthood had to be changed from the inferior Levitical Priesthood to the superior Melchizedek Priesthood.

Example of a Texan Great-grandfather

This law of heredity is further illustrated by a Texas history lesson. In 1820, Moses Austin received an empresario grant from the government of Mexico to settle the northern province of Cohuila y Tejas (modern-day Texas). After his death, his son Stephen F. Austin pursued his father's dream of establishing a colony in the area. In accordance with the grant, Stephen F. Austin recruited three hundred families to the colony. These families settled in an area south and west of Houston, which later became the beginning of the State of Texas. These families were mainly of Irish, Scottish, and English descent.

According to my calculations, my great-grandfather who lived in Bristol, England, and was working as a laborer in the Bristol dockyard would have been in his early twenties at that time. Let's just imagine that he responded when Stephen F. Austin was recruiting those three hundred families. Imagine that he decided to be one of those original immigrant families and sailed across to America in 1825. Like everybody else, he would have been given an allocation of four thousand acres of rich Texas land as a gift, which he would have farmed with his family.

Imagine that, years later, his descendants also discovered that underneath that rich farming land there were significant oil reserves. My great-grandfather's descendants would then have become Texan multimillionaires because of the oil. This actually happened to some of those three hundred original families that settled in Austin's colony.

But just think for a moment! If my great-grandfather had made that decision to emigrate to Texas, how would it have affected me? Instead of being born in England, I would have been born in Texas and probably would have become a multimillionaire. I would be oozing with money and talking with a good old Texan drawl as opposed to my British accent.

But my great-grandfather, if he ever heard of this opportunity, decided not to go and remained a poor dock laborer in Bristol, England. His decision not to go seriously affected not only his future but also my future because I was in his loins, although still unborn by three generations. As a result, I was involved with him in that decision not to go to America. So instead of being born a rich Texan, I was born a poor Brit!

This Law of Heredity and Inherited Sin

In a similar way, because we are all descendants of Adam and Eve, their sin was manifested in our lives from birth. This, again, proves the law of heredity. This sin is sometimes called original sin. Applying the law of heredity, we see that all of us were actually "in Adam" and involved with him in his action when he chose to sin. So, through our ancestor, Adam, the consequences of his actions and his sin passed on to all of his descendants. As stated in Romans 5:12, "through one man sin entered the world, and death through sin, thus death spread to all men because all sinned." Through Adam, sin passed to each one of us because we were actually "in him" and participating in his act of disobedience.

In Adam, this hereditary line manifests as hereditary sin, generational curses, hereditary diseases, family curses, witchcraft, and occult practices. Hereditary sin can also occur due to tribal ceremonies and national and regional curses placed upon us through our ancestors. In addition, participation in false sects and Christ-less religions can also manifest generational curses. Cultural traditions such as ancestral worship and veneration of the dead open the door to demonic curses.

Only the power of the Cross can deliver us from these hereditary and generational curses because Jesus became a curse for us (see Gal. 3:13). The benefit of the Cross, which has the power to break all of these curses, has to be applied specifically by faith.

The Law of Heredity and Christ

This same law of heredity works gloriously for us in Christ. This sinful nature and cursed inheritance in Adam was taken away in the Cross and is now replaced with the glorious new nature of the Risen Christ. The law of heredity now works wonderfully for us because of our inheritance in Christ (see Rom. 5:15–21).

In Christ, we are delivered completely from the power of Satan and any curses placed upon us by those who hate us or who hated our ancestors. We are freed from any cursed things our ancestors brought upon themselves and upon us by their occult practices.

Additionally, a careful study of Romans 6:1–5 indicates we were actually in Christ when He became sin and when He paid the full penalty for sin. We were in Him when He was buried. We were in Him when He was raised from the dead and in Him when he sat down on His throne with all power and authority. The phrase "in Him" or "together with Him" comes frequently in the epistles especially in Romans, Ephesians, and Colossians. In the same way, we were in sin through the law of heredity in Adam; through that same law, we have been made dead to sin and alive to God in Christ Jesus (see Rom. 6:5, Eph. 2:4–6).

The Nature of Christ's Death

There in the garden of Gethsemane, the Father handed Jesus a cup. This cup represented all the sin of all Adam's race from the beginning to the end of time. Jesus fully drank the cup and took into His body all that sin, carrying it to the Cross: "He who knew no sin became sin for us" in body and soul (2 Cor. 5:21). His body was the receptacle for all the sin of Adam's race and His soul was the receptacle for the sinful nature.

The Bible teaches us that the sting of death is sin (1 Cor. 15:56). On the Cross, Jesus was cursed with the sting of death more deeply than any man. He became the last Adam, the focal point, the concentrated garbage container, the refuse pit for all the sin of Adam's race from the beginning to the end of time (1 Cor. 15:15). All of this was concentrated into that cup that He drank! No wonder He recoiled from drinking it and cried out, "Oh my Father, if it is possible let this cup pass from me" (Matt 26:39), but it was not possible—He had to drink it—so He did.

On the Cross, God poured out His full wrath against all the sin of Adam's race upon Jesus as the last Adam. It was God who bruised Him. It was God who chastised Him. On the Cross, while sin was being paid for, fellowship between the Father and the Son was totally broken. It was God who put Jesus to grief and punished Him in this way. The Jews and the Roman soldiers were simply the instruments of God's wrath (Isa. 53:3–11, Ps. 22:1–31). When His suffering was complete, Jesus cried out with a loud cry, "It is finished." It was a cry of triumph not pain. Sin was now fully paid for. Jesus immediately dismissed His Spirit and physically died.

The Roman Centurion, who crucified Jesus, was so stunned to see Jesus totally in charge of His own execution, even choosing for Himself the moment of His death, that the soldier knelt down, bowed his head, and said, "Truly this man was the Son of God" (Mark 15:39). And at the same moment Jesus died, the veil of the Temple was ripped open from top to bottom (Mark 15:38), signifying that the way into the Holy of Holies was now open to all believers.

As a glorious demonstration that death and sin had been completely conquered, the tombs of some believers who had already died were opened, and they began to walk around Jerusalem. But there was even more to come.

CHAPTER 5

A New Heredity in Christ

The law of heredity worked invincibly against us in Adam as described in Romans 5, but in Romans 6, we are suddenly shown a new glorious truth about this law—namely, that it also worked powerfully for us in Christ.

Jesus obtained his resurrection by faith as He prayed in the Garden of Gethsemane before He even went to the Cross (Heb. 5:7). He prayed to be delivered "out from within death," and He was. Hallelujah! Very early on that resurrection morning, He was raised from the dead by the glory of the Father (Rom. 6:4). What God did at the Cross was to cut us off from that hereditary line in Adam and graft us into a new hereditary line in Christ. When Jesus was on the Cross, because of that glorious law of hereditary, you and I were in His loins and therefore involved with Him in His act of propitiating the wrath of God. This makes it possible for God to righteously and joyfully forgive us for all our sins. Can you see where this is leading?

I now understand that when Jesus died, although I did not exist, I was in Him. The law of heredity worked horribly against me in Adam, but it worked gloriously for me in Christ. Hallelujah!

I was born with the nature of sin after the flesh through Adam. It was not just a theological position; it was absolutely real. I didn't just theologically reckon myself to have a nasty nature; I actually had one because of that ancestry. And so did you, if you are honest with yourself. I didn't just theologically have a bad temper; I really had a bad temper. I didn't have a theological unclean mind; I had an unclean mind. I didn't have theological anger; I had real anger. It was real, because it was a real inheritance through Adam.

Can you see how it works against us in our lineage through Adam? However, it also works gloriously for us in our lineage after Christ! If you can really grasp this, something will explode in your spirit. When God says that you and I were united together with Christ in His death (Rom. 6:5), that is exactly what He means. When He says you and I were buried together with Christ, that is exactly what He means. When He says you and I were raised together with Christ (Rom. 6:4, Col. 2:12), that is exactly what He means. You and I were "in the loins" of Christ participating with Him in everything He did.

Finally, when He ascended to the Father and sat down at the right hand of the throne of God, you and I were also there in the loins of Christ, participating with Him as He received all the glorious benefits of His obedience. We now share them with Him forever. Hallelujah! I know this will take a while to soak in, but let this grip your spirit as you realize that God has done that glorious thing for us in Christ.

Just as the risen Christ is righteous, upon your confession of faith in Christ, you, too, were made righteous. The law of heredity has to be possessed by faith. God has cut you and me off from Adam's genealogy and grafted us into a new genealogy, the righteousness of Christ. That is what Christ has done for us on the Cross.

We Are Baptized into Christ

Romans 6:3 says, "Or do you not know that as many of us as were baptized into Christ Jesus were baptized into His death." The Bible has used baptism as a means of experiencing Christ's death and resurrection; we are baptized into Christ. We are united with Him in baptism. When we are baptized, we are symbolically buried in the waters of baptism, which is why immersion is the obvious and only satisfactory way to be baptized. You have to be plunged beneath the waters of baptism as a believer to enter into the death that He died. But you are not left there under the water indefinitely. You are raised again! Baptism is an act that God has chosen to seal this truth. It is a physical act of obedience, which is a deep spiritual mystery. If you come into baptism by faith, then the spiritual power of it will work in your life.

Why was Jesus baptized? He didn't have any sins to wash away. He did not have an old sinful nature to bury. His baptism was a baptism of identification. He came down into the waters of the river Jordan, where Adam's race was seeking the solution to their sins. John the Baptist was baptizing the people into repentance, a forerunner until the Cross had done its work.

The Bible tells us that multitudes were sincerely seeking a solution to their sins; they came to John because they wanted to repent and be baptized. I can imagine that sometimes they had to wait hours to step down into the Jordon River, yet they continued to wait as John exhorted them to change their ways. Now imagine the Lord Jesus joining the crowd and waiting in line to also step down into the water and be baptized by John. Here, Jesus was the answer to all that sin. Here came the sin bearer, Jesus, the Christ. When Jesus was baptized, he had no sins to be forgiven; he had no need for repentance, but symbolically He came to the deepest place of man's degradation and was baptized into Adam's race. Though born of Mary, the complete identification with Adam's race took place in the waters of the river Jordan. Jesus was totally identified with Adam's race through his immersion. Although he never inherited a sinful nature, His humanity was the same as ours apart from the sinful nature. Jesus, the Son of man, was baptized into that Adamic nature, and it became part of Him yet though tempted in every manner just as we are, He was without sin.

We can use another metaphor. The baptism of Jesus was like a wedding service. Imagine the Father of the Bridegroom saying to his Son, "Will You marry this fallen, sin-ridden, corrupt, and wicked race of Adam? Will You marry into her family and become her Husband? Then, as a family member from within the family, will You be her Kinsman-Redeemer and pay all her debts on her behalf? Will you then gloriously cleanse her with the water of the Word and transform her into a spotless Bride and present her faultless before Me?"

In His baptism, the Son replied, "Oh, Father, I will!" Therefore, by His baptism Jesus conducted a public testimony to His act of marrying Adam's race. When we come to baptism, we are completing the other half of the wedding service. When we come as individuals to Jesus, then the Father of the Bridegroom says to us, "Will you receive this Man to be your lawfully wedded husband? Will you honor Him, obey Him, and serve Him?" We must respond, "Oh, Father, I will!"

In baptism, we are married to Christ. Hallelujah! Those who come to Christ in faith receive all His riches, all His wealth, His great Name, all His personal power, and all His glory. Baptism into Him is like a marriage. As we learn and understand the depth of the meaning of baptism, we are amazed at the length the Lord Jesus went to save us. Of course, we want to declare our faith in Him by being baptized. Every time I see a baptism, I want to "go down" and do it all over again, but it is only necessary once and never needs to be repeated.

In Romans 6:4 and Colossians 2:12, we have another truth. When we are baptized into Christ, we are baptized into His death. What made His death so unique? When the moment came for Jesus to actually become the Savior of the world, it was necessary for the Father to take all the sins of Adam's race from the beginning to the end of time and lay it all on Him. Every sin that any man and any woman had ever committed or would commit was gathered together and heaped upon Him. The totality of all sin from the beginning to the end of Adam's race was laid upon him. Think about this! Pray and let the Lord enable you to receive this revelation.

You cannot carry the full weight of it because it would probably crush you. We all need to meditate on these things and grasp the enormity of His burden.

There was a time, years ago, when I was ministering to a man who was badly demon-possessed. He had participated in every kind of sexual perversion possible. This depraved man was desperately seeking help. He had finally come to Christ, but the demons were not going to let go of him so easily.

As we were ministering to him for several hours, I felt the absolute depravity emanating from the demons in him and washing over me, making me feel unclean and filthy. It's difficult even to explain. For a period of time, while helping this man, I felt waves of what it feels like to be a homosexual wash over me. The demons were like dirt that clung to me.

Late in the night, as we battled on for several hours, the presence of Jesus filled the room. He simply spoke a word. The demons all fled. They all came out of the man and he was free; it was all over. I went straight to my room to take a shower. I felt I wanted to wash and wash to get clean. The filthiness of these few demons in this one man was enough to contaminate and revolt me. I began to think what it must have been like for Jesus when the sin of the whole world, every single evil act of Adam's race, was laid upon him. No wonder He cried out, "Father, if it be possible let this cup pass from Me, nevertheless, not My will but Your will be done" (Matt. 26:39).

Jesus Carried All Our Sin

In 1 Corinthians 15:45-47, Jesus is described as the Last Adam, a life-giving spirit, the Lord from heaven. Jesus, the Son of Man, bearing our humanity and baptized into Adam's race, became "the Last Adam"—"last" because Jesus took all of "Adam's race" to the Cross, died for it, and paid for the sin and rebellion with His precious blood for all humanity. There He birthed a new generation—Sons of God, no longer sons of Adam. As the substitutionary sacrifice to God for humankind's sin, His body became like a garbage can into which God dumped all the sinful refuse and filth of Adam's race. God pushed it all on Jesus. All the foul depravity and obscenity of Adam's race was laid upon Christ. The travail of Gethsemane was the horror of bearing all that sin. It was not the physical suffering that He was about to experience that most concerned Him. Rather, it was the revulsion of taking all the sin of Adam's race upon Himself and literally being made sin for us. Jesus said, "If it be possible let this cup pass from Me, but not My will, Yours be done," and He submitted to the Father's will and drank the cup, the symbol of all of Adam's sin. This was the cup of His suffering.

In addition to this, please notice what is said in 2 Corinthians 5:21, "For He made Him who knew no sin to be sin for us, that we might become the righteousness of God in Him." This is an even greater mystery. Not only did the acts of sin come upon Jesus, but the very nature of sin was somehow laid upon Him. He was made sin for us and sin itself somehow became part of Him.

The Unique Resurrection of Jesus

When the disciples burst forth from the upper room in the power of the Spirit on the Day of Pentecost, the Bible says they went everywhere preaching the resurrection of the Lord Jesus, and we have to understand why. They did not just preach about it on Easter Sunday. It was the constant passion of their lives. They never went anywhere preaching the raising of Lazarus from the dead although the raising of Lazarus was a greater physical miracle. How long was Lazarus in the tomb? The Bible says that Lazarus was in the tomb for four days (John 11:17). How long was Jesus dead? The scripture continually testifies that after His crucifixion He would rise up from the dead on the third day, and He did (Matt. 16:21, 17:23, 20:19, 27:63; Luke 24:7, 21, 46; 1 Cor. 15:4)! What happened to Lazarus's body? Unlike Christ, his body suffered corruption. What happened to Jesus's body? God didn't permit it to suffer corruption.

The power of the Cross is not simply in the physical fact of Jesus's death and resurrection. It is centered in the kind of death He died and in the power of His resurrection. No one has ever died like Jesus. No one ever will. It says in Hebrews 2:9 that Jesus tasted death on behalf of every man. The Bible also says in 1 Corinthians 15:56 that the sting of death is sin—the more you are stung with sin, the more agonizing will be that death. Jesus was stung by sin more than any other man and went down into death more deeply than any man millions of times over.

As Jesus hung on the Cross, He was bearing in His body the sins of the whole of Adam's race. He was also bearing in His body the very nature of sin. He became the foulest, filthiest, most sin-laden man the world has ever seen. But it was not His sin; it was everybody else's sin. Can you see what a claim death had upon Him? The sting of death is sin—how deeply it must have stung Him!

As death opened its jaws to swallow Him up, it dragged Him down into the deepest depths of dying. Because of the weight of sin, death had more right and claim upon Him than over any other human being.

Delivered "Out from Within" Death

However, we need to understand another amazing truth. Jesus had already obtained His resurrection by an act of warring faith in the Garden of Gethsemane even before He went to the Cross and died.

I want to bring you to the truth and power of the Cross as presented in the book of Hebrews. In Hebrews 5:7, the writer is talking about Jesus as Melchizedek when he says,

> *who, in the days of His Flesh, when He had offered up prayers and supplications, with vehement cries and tears to Him who was able to save Him from (literally "out from within") death, and was heard because of His godly fear*

Now that verse puzzled me for years until I looked more carefully into the Greek manuscript. There is one little preposition in this verse that unlocks the power of this mystery. In the Greek manuscript, there are just two letters *ek* in this preposition. It is a preposition that has movement. It literally means "to come out from within something." It means to be inside something and then be moved by an external force to come outside what you were formerly inside of. I do not know why the translators fail to clearly translate it in this way because they miss a powerful point of truth.

Jesus was not saying that He wanted to be saved from death. He did not pray, "Oh, Father, I don't want to die." Instead, He was praying, "Father, when I have died, I claim that death, which will have such a claim on me, will not be able to hold Me. Death and Hades will have more right to drag me down to the depths of hell than any other man. The power of this death will be more than any other human being has ever experienced, but at Your Word, I am claiming by the power and glory of the Father I will be raised up out from within this death!" and He was heard! Hallelujah (Rom. 6:4; see also Eph. 1:19–20)!

Jesus already had the title deed to His resurrection even before He died because of His prayer of faith upon the Word of His Father. He had obtained the title deed as He prayed in the Garden of Gethsemane. He was not going to remain dead but was going deep down into death and would come up out from within death by the power and glory of the Father. When we understand the nature of His death, then we begin to understand the power of what really happened at the Cross.

As Jesus went down into death on the Cross, He cried out, "My God, my God, why have you forsaken me" (Matt. 27:46; Ps. 22:1–31)? As we have already seen, the reason He cried this cry was because He was at that time the filthiest, most sin-laden man the world had ever seen. The Father could have no fellowship with Him in that condition. A gap as wide as Hades opened between Father and Son while He was bearing the sin of Adam's race. He was absolutely alone. Can you imagine that? When He needed his Father the most, He was cut off from Him.

Jesus was surrounded during those terrible hours of suffering by jubilant demons, mocking men, the darkness of Hades, and the physical pain and agony of the suffering of the Cross. But even in that condition, Jesus was fighting the good fight of faith to obtain His resurrection and your salvation. In so doing, He would redeem all of creation, bring forth the Church, and save the Nations. What a Savior!

Jesus never felt sorry for Himself, even on the Cross. He fought a glorious battle of faith, and He won! Just imagine a scenario something like this:

> On the third day, Hades began to shake. I can just imagine the demons on duty saying, "Hey, what's going on around here? Everything is shaking!"
> Then quickly the alarm bells went off, and a terrified demon shouted out, "There is a prisoner breaking out!"
> "Who is it?" shouted another.
> "It's the Son of Man!" someone cried out.
> "Him? It's impossible for Him to rise!" said another.
> "There is a power coming against me that I cannot resist" shouted another.

The scriptures say Jesus "divested" Himself of principalities and powers. They were still trying to cling to Him like leeches as He rose. I can see Jesus majestically rising from death with these things still hanging on to Him and crying out, "Oh, don't let Him rise! Stop him!"

As He rose "out from within death," I can imagine Jesus saying, "Get off Me you filthy things! You can't have Me! You can't stop Me! Be gone!" They were stripped off Him by the power and glory of the Father, and He ascended to the glorious Third Heaven to sit at the Father's right hand. Was there any sin left sticking to Him in His resurrection? Absolutely not!

He died with millions of bad tempers, millions of unclean minds, and every kind of filthiness and obscenity upon Him. But in His resurrection they were all completely gone!

Let us go back to Lazarus. When he died, he died with a normal amount of human sin. We don't know what Lazarus was like, but let's imagine that he had a bit of a bad temper or other character defects. Regardless, when Lazarus died he had certain human weaknesses that were part of his personality just like you and me. When he was raised from the dead and came out of the tomb alive, it was the same Lazarus with the same personality and weaknesses that had gone into the tomb. Nothing had changed.

The resurrection of Lazarus from the dead was an amazing physical miracle but, the resurrection of Jesus was by the Glory of the Father. Jesus's resurrection was a demonstration of the exceeding greatness of the Father's power to raise Him not only physically but also spiritually and morally clean. In the death of Jesus all the foulness, obscenity, and degradation of Adam's race was concentrated in Him. Yet when He rose, all sin was gone! He rose as a totally new creation. Now there was nothing but the pure perfection of His Eternal Life. Hallelujah!

United in Death and Resurrection

We can now understand what Paul is telling us in Romans 6:4, "Therefore we were buried with Him through baptism into death, that just as Christ was raised from the dead by the glory of the Father, even so we also should walk in newness of life." If you can see an unclean mind or any filthiness in the risen Jesus, then you can excuse it in your own life. Otherwise it has to be gone. This is a matter of faith. You can appropriate this reality in your life through the power of the Cross. Notice what Paul says in the next verse, "For if we have been united together in the likeness of His death then we shall certainly also be *in the likeness of His* resurrection" (Rom. 6:5).

The King James and New King James versions of the Bible inserted the italic words you see in Romans 6:5. These words are not in the original Greek manuscript. The translators have added these words believing they help to bring clarity, but in this case, they do not clarify the meaning. The original Greek is very strong here.

We already *are* His resurrection. Romans 6:5 literally says: "If we have been united in the likeness of His death, certainly also we (already) are His resurrection." We are not in the "likeness of His resurrection"; "we already are His resurrection." This is not a future event but a present reality in Christ.

2 Corinthians 5:17 is a similar verse that has this kind of declaration, like a newspaper boy calling out the headlines on the street corner, when he shouts out the latest most important news headline. A literal paraphrase would be: "Any man in Christ? He's a new creation" (2 Cor. 5:17)!

In Bombay, India, where I lived for many years, you could go into the large and fascinating Crawford Marketplace. As well as the big stores, there were also many little market stalls where you could buy an assortment of items. One of these stalls sold what looked like very nice Schaeffer pens allegedly manufactured in the United States of America. The actual genuine Schaeffer pens were fairly expensive and of high quality. One day, while strolling among these little stalls I was surprised to find some Schaeffer pens being sold for only three US dollars each. I picked up a pen and found stamped on the side "Made in USA." However, what they didn't tell me was that the initials "USA" stood for the Ulasnagar-Sindhi-Association. In villages outside Bombay, people were working in little huts, making convincing imitations of the real thing, but they didn't have the quality or the lasting power of the real thing. It looked all right until you tried to use it, and then it broke and did not work.

Many people have this attitude to the resurrection of Jesus Christ. They don't really expect it to work for them. Even some translators don't really believe it, so they have watered down what the scriptures actually say. It seems too strong for them to say we actually are His resurrection, but that is what the original manuscript says. That is what God meant when he told Paul to write these words. Paraphrased, they would read, "You have been truly united in a death like His and you actually are His resurrection."

God dealt as radically with the sin in your life as He did with the sin that was put upon Jesus. It is a matter of faith to realize your riches in Christ Jesus. We have to believe what God says even when we do not necessarily understand it. My mind may not be able to understand it, but my spirit can rejoice in the truth of the revelation. Given time, my spirit will instruct my intellect in the power and depth of the revelation of the Cross. For example, you may reason saying, "How can I be a new creation? It is not happening. I still have many problems. I am still battling with smoking. I still shout at the kids. I am irritable. How can I really have resurrection in life?"

It is very simple: you must decide to believe it because God says He has accomplished it. As you persistently lay hold of God's revelation by faith, it will progressively become an actual manifestation in your life. The power of the Cross can then do its full work in you.

Our Old Man Was Crucified

We already know what happened to Jesus when He died. We also know one thing that happened to us when Jesus rose again. Now we need to learn a second truth regarding our new life. Romans 6:6 states, "Knowing this, that our old man is crucified with Him, that the body of sin might be done away with, that we should no longer be slaves to sin."

The phrase "done away with" is a strong phrase. The various commentators argue about what the Greek actually says. Once again, their interpretation waters down the scripture. They question how the old man could really be destroyed when in many lives it still seems to be alive and active. However, the Greek word here is very strong. It means "to render utterly powerless" or "to have been destroyed" just as if it had disappeared. We are told here that the power of the Cross is able to crucify the old man once and for all so that it never troubles us again!

In the first work of the Cross, Jesus died for me. That is a once and for all act. He died only once and He does not have to continue offering additional sacrifices for sin. His one death upon the Cross was sufficient for all sin, for all men, and for all of time because we were all there in Him. There never will be any need for Him to do it again.

Don't receive the wrong teaching that says, "Oh, Jesus died to pay for all your past sins, but not your future sins." That is simply not true! All our sins—past, present, and future—were in Him when He died. The Cross is not only an event of time; it is an event of eternity. It happened at a particular point in time, but it has an eternal effect that reaches from the beginning to the end of time.

Abraham could look forward about two thousand years and receive the power of the Cross and live in that power during his days on earth. King David could look forward about one thousand years and receive the same power of the Cross and live by it. The apostle Paul could look back a few years and receive the power of the Cross and live by it. Martin Luther could look back fifteen hundred years and receive the power of the Cross and live in it as a present reality. You and I can look back about two thousand years and receive the same power of the Cross and live by it today.

The Three Strands of the Old Man

Let me say something here about the true nature of the New Birth. In Psalm 51:5, David says, "Behold, I was brought forth in iniquity, and in sin my mother conceived me." David was not insulting his mother's morality for the way he was brought into the world. Instead, he recognized that by being born of a woman he received the Adamic sinful nature as part of his being, but David also says that he was "shaped in iniquity." This refers to the way his parents raised and treated him. It includes his experiences in life, the way the other people treated him such as his elder brothers and of course King Saul, whom he had tried to serve faithfully for many years.

All kinds of experiences have caused all of us to be shaped by the iniquity of the world into which we were born and have lived for years. Maybe you have a terrible fear and insecurity in you because of your parent's demeaning remarks. "Don't do that! You'll never be any good. I didn't want you and I wish you had never been born!" Words like that are like wounding arrows shot into the soul. We become wounded by the rejection of those statements. We are shaped by their iniquity.

Sometimes kids have to travel to school on the school bus, and all the other kids make fun of them on the bus. They mock the new glasses; they might be wearing braces on their teeth or they are possibly overweight. The other kids make jabbing statements like "Hey, Fatso!" As a result, we learn not to go out and play with the other children. Instead, we stay in the school building hiding because we don't want them to mock us. We are being shaped by iniquity. Maybe you had a bad teacher who didn't like you and said, "You'll never make it. You'll never be any good." As a result, you received the idea that you were a failure while still a small child. Many of us have experienced these things to different degrees. You may have been abused sexually by a parent, the very people who should have loved and protected you. Such a violation is a shocking degradation that can hardly be comprehended. Many are shaped by such iniquity.

The third and final dimension of our old man is what we ourselves have done. We cannot blame everything on the Devil or our forefathers or our associates or our parents. You and I have also made choices of our own that have created deeply ingrained habits of sin in our lives.

So when we come to salvation, we already have this three-stranded old man formed in us. We have the iniquity we were born with through our Adamic inheritance; we have the iniquity of our natural heredity line, those who influenced our lives; and we have the iniquity of sinful habits caused by decisions we have made in our life. That is the old man.

We are told here in Romans 6:6 that God took that old man and rendered him powerless. He destroyed the old man. He did not patch it up. He did not try to repair it. He did not try to improve it. He crucified it in Christ and took it away.

In the first work of the Cross, Jesus died for me. In the second work of the Cross, I died together with Jesus! In dying with Him, I experience the crucifixion of my old man because I am now in Christ. The result is that my old man is destroyed. It is rendered completely powerless.

My wife, Eileen, has testified to the reality of this power. We were then missionaries in India and were attending a conference in a city called Nasik, where a wonderful man of God spoke on the power of the Cross. But I will let Eileen tell it in her own words from her book *Faith Works, a True Story of Radical Obedience:*

> When we learned that David McKee was to be the speaker at meetings in a city about 125 miles from Bombay, it took no time for both the Hutchinson's and ourselves to rearrange appointments and go. David preached powerfully from Romans chapter six, about knowing ourselves dead to sin and alive unto God. Interestingly, John Hutchinson had been going through the same

passage during our weekly Bible studies. These had deeply challenged me but at the same time I was frustrated. One day I said, "Lord I have tried to be dead to myself till I'm 'blue in the face,' but all I discover is that I am very much alive!"

David McKee told a story of a preacher who dug a hole in the garden. He then invited his congregation to come and bury their old selves by faith. He stressed our need to believe the Bible and not our feelings. God was speaking to the depths of my being. It is one thing to have faith for finance, but now, I needed a revelation of how to have faith for victory over sin. I wanted unshakable faith to know myself dead to sin and alive unto God. The words at the end of Matthew 5, "Be perfect therefore as your Father in Heaven is perfect" always troubled me. How can I live this kind of life?

Sitting on the back of Alan's motorbike, going home after the meeting, I was pondering all these things. Suddenly the truth became reality as it hit my heart. I believed the Word. Right there on the back of the motorbike I said, "I know I died with Christ and now I live with Him. Lord, I believe; I reckon myself dead, really dead to sin and alive unto God. Sin shall not have dominion over me. I praise You Lord!" Then by faith, I threw my old self over the hedge somewhere between Deolali and Nasik! It was done and I was rejoicing. I didn't need to understand; I knew and I believed.

I didn't seem to be any different the next day. I hadn't suddenly turned into a sinless saint! If I had wanted to doubt, I had plenty of opportunity. The Lord led me to understand that by deciding to believe God's word, He had begun a process in me. Over the following weeks and months He began to work the truth into the fabric of my life just as I had believed.

Did you notice that Eileen said, "He had begun a process in me"? Let me repeat: there is a crisis of faith where we believe the Word of God—"I died with Christ," and "sin shall not have dominion over me." Then the glorious truth is worked into our lives by a process of continuing faith.

The Power of the Cross to Destroy the Old Man

Hear me! There is power in that Cross to destroy the old man. This is for every one of us. But you must get hold of God for it. It is worth pursuing with all your heart. Ask for it and cry out for it and it will be yours.

According to the scripture, what happens if you ask? Jesus said, "ask and it will be given to you; seek, and you will find; knock, and the door will be opened to you. For everyone who asks receives; and he who seeks finds; and to him who knocks, it will be opened" (Luke 11:9–10). This six-fold guarantee from Jesus assures us that if we go after this truth we will obtain it. God does not say these things in His Word to torment us. He says these things because they are true. There is a power in the Cross to slay the old man. You do not have to be a prisoner to your hereditary past, your parental past, or your personal past.

I rejected Christianity in my teenage years and early twenties. I read books and watched films that absolutely polluted my mind. I never committed a wrong sexual act with anyone physically, but in my mind, I did so a number of times. I thought, *When I get married I will be free from all these wrong thoughts and be cured from all of this pollution*, but it didn't happen.

Even after I became a Christian, I continued with habits that I would be ashamed to tell you about. I still struggled with this lusting, unclean mind for several years until I saw from scripture that God had promised, through the power of the Cross, to give me in this life the very mind of Christ. My spirit leapt within me, and I violently grabbed hold of that promise by faith. Then the Cross was able to do its liberating work in me, and the tyranny of that sinful and lustful mind was broken once and for all.

Through the Cross, God gave me a new pure mind. As He had promised, He gave me the mind of Christ. I am very careful with this new mind and guard what the Father has given to me. There is a mighty power in the Cross to destroy the old man and I am rejoicing in it. Hallelujah!

Let me summarize this teaching. First, we need to know that we were baptized into Christ's death and the old man was destroyed. Paul explains this in Romans 6:9–10, which I paraphrase here:

> *For we know that since Christ was raised from the dead, He cannot die again; death no longer has mastery over Him. The death*

He died, He died to sin once and for all, but the life He lives, He lives to God.

You and I can live to God just as Jesus lived to God when the Cross has done its work in us. You must grab hold of this, the same way you received your salvation. You receive every work of the Cross by faith. It is written to be possessed by the believer.

The second work of the Cross is me dying with Christ once and for all to put to death the old man. It is finished! The old man is rendered completely powerless, no longer having any power over me. Therefore, I do not have to continue in sin. I can be freed from its power, so let us praise God. What a Savior! To seal this truth, pray this prayer:

Thank you, Lord Jesus, for the way You dealt with the old man on the Cross. I pray that the truth of the message of the Cross will do its mighty work in me. Set me free to be the new creature that I am in Christ. I pray that You will increase the spirit of faith upon me. I want to believe the Word, not just hear it.

Father, I receive faith in my heart for these words to become my reality, not a mirage, not a myth but the solid truth of God's Word. Give me the grace to get hold of this truth. I will not tolerate the sub-Christian experience of continuing in sin. I thank You for hearing me and granting this prayer. In Jesus's Name, Amen.

CHAPTER 6

THE POWER OF THE CROSS TO CRUCIFY THE FLESH

What then? Shall we sin because we are not under law but under grace? By no means! (Rom. 6:15)

The Flesh versus the Old Man

The fact that Jesus went to the Cross is the center of everything. In this chapter, I want to talk about the power of the Cross to deal with what the Bible calls "the flesh." (The NIV and many modern translations use the phrase "sinful nature.")

If we do not make the distinction between the "old man" and the "flesh," then we will miss the victory that God wants us to live in. We have certain spiritual enemies, and the Bible has prescribed specific weapons or solutions to deal with those enemies. Similarly, if we apply the wrong remedy to the wrong disease, we will not be healed.

The Cross renders the old man powerless because he was crucified with Christ. We are liberated from the tyranny of the old man when we put our faith in Jesus's crucifixion on the Cross, but this does not automatically bring us into victorious Christian living. Instead, we are now free to choose who our master will be.

Mankind was created by God to live under God's ruling authority. We were created by God to live voluntarily under the loving "Father" rule of God. That is how Adam and Eve lived before they sinned. They lived a perfect, sinless life not because of any power within them to do so, but because of the power that flowed into them from God. While they lived in obedience and submission to God, the power of God's eternal life filled their lives, causing them to live in sinless victory. All of creation also lived in peaceful order under the benefit of Adam and Eve's rule.

Man was designed by God to be a dependent being. The possibility of a man successfully living an independent life is a lie of the Devil. When the Devil persuades someone to step out from under the benevolent rule of God into independence, they immediately become the victim of Satan's rule instead. No man has the ability to live an independent life.

Ephesians 2:1–3 explains that if you are not under the rule of God, then Satan, the "ruler of the kingdom of the air," is at work in you:

And you He made alive, who were dead in trespasses and sins, in which you once walked according to the course of this world, according to the prince of the power of the air, the spirit who now works in the sons of disobedience, among whom also we all once conducted ourselves in the lusts of our flesh, fulfilling the desires of the flesh and of the mind, and were by nature children of wrath, just as the others.

You cannot stop the world from shaping you. You will automatically become a product of those demonic forces that rule the air until there is a change of rulership in your life. If you are not living under the rule of God, then all of these influences: the world, your unsaved peers, and your own flesh, are controlled by the Devil. Therefore, you end up doing the will of the Devil without even realizing it or wanting to.

For the first twenty-eight years of my life, I only cared about myself. I thought I was free, independent, and directing my own life, but that was actually a lie and a deception. All the time, like a puppet, I was being controlled by the Devil. I was under the power of the prince of this world and did not realize it. That is true of everyone until Jesus becomes their Lord.

We Cannot Continue in Sin

While the Cross puts to death the old man, breaking its tyranny in our life, we now have the freedom to choose whom we will allow to rule over us. This choice must be made consciously and on a continuous basis.

The Christian life is not supposed to be a life of constant sinning and then going to God each day to ask for forgiveness for our failure. Paul instructs in Romans 6:15, "What then? Shall we continue in sin because we are not under law but under grace? [By no means!]," and in Romans 6:1-2, "What shall we say then? Shall we continue in sin that grace may abound? Certainly not! How shall we who died to sin live any longer in it?" The power of the Cross gives us the ability to stop sinning.

The expectation that we will always sin is the typical teaching of some Jewish and Christian denominations. It has its roots in traditional Judaism and is not of the Kingdom of God. Many Christian people think it is normal to live a week of failure and then to confess those sins on Sunday, take communion, and receive prayer from the priest, who pronounces that they are forgiven. They believe their sins of the past week are washed away and then they return to their normal life to sin again in the new week. Many churches teach a fatalism of permanent sinfulness and that the blood of Jesus is there only to cover another week of sinning. That is not the Gospel.

Do Paul's words in Romans indicate that the Gospel of Jesus Christ only has the power to reduce the amount of sinning in our life rather than completely eradicate it? This is an important question! And to use his words to respond to this question, "By no means. Absolutely not!"

Some might reason that before I was saved I used to swear twenty times a day, but now I only occasionally swear. Before I was saved I used to hit my wife every day, but now I only hit her occasionally. Great improvement! But this is not the Gospel of Jesus Christ! However, this is the way many believers actually live. They expect the Gospel to bring a reduction of sin, but the idea of not sinning seems almost like heresy to them. Our ability to live without sinning is exactly what the Bible teaches (see John 1:7).

I am not suggesting that there is an automatic, permanent condition of sinless perfection in this life. However, the Bible certainly teaches us that there is power in the Cross to enable us to not sin. The power of the Cross breaks the tyranny of the "old man" and allows you to make important choices every day. For the first time in your life, you have the ability to exercise freedom of choice. You can choose either to submit to the rule of the Spirit of God and obey Him, just like Jesus did, or you can still give in and submit to the rule of sin. You can either let righteousness rule over you or you can choose to do your own independent thing and let sin rule over you instead. You now have the opportunity to choose to whom you are going to yield the members of your body to obey. As reflected in 1 Corinthians 10:30, "No temptation has overtaken you except what is common to mankind. And God is faithful; he will not let you be tempted beyond what you can bear. But when you are tempted he will also provide a way out so that you can endure it."

In other words, the message is: "Choose your master!" You cannot be free to do your own thing. You can only choose who will rule over you: Satan or God. If you choose God to rule over you, then there is a possibility of not sinning. To choose otherwise is to allow the world to rule over you, and you will go on sinning.

The Flesh Is Weak

Now I want to give you a good definition of the flesh. The "flesh" is that union of body and soul that acts independently of God. The old man is a wicked rebel against God. It has a hatred of God and His righteousness. The old man has been crucified with Christ. However, the flesh is always with us and is not wicked but simply weak.

The flesh does not want to sin. In fact, it tries hard not to sin, but when it relies on its own strength to stop sinning it always fails. That is the difference between the "flesh" and the "old man." The old man says, "I won't obey God's laws! I hate God and His ways. I hate God and His righteousness! I am a rebel against all these things!" The flesh says, "I'll try and be good. I will seriously strive to do well. I really want to live a better life. I'm going to give my best effort to change!"

The flesh will fail, not through rebellion as the old man does but through weakness. Can you see the difference? It is impossible out of the strength of our own self-life to try and live a victorious Christian life. Many try to build the discipline of the soul and the discipline of the body in order to overcome the weakness of the flesh, but therein lies the greatest weakness. The weakness of the flesh is self-effort!

Everything to do with the flesh is self—self-effort and self-gratification. The trouble with the flesh is that it is one great big "I." It even says, "I will do my best to try to serve God," but it is impossible to do so in its own strength.

When I went to India as a missionary, although God called me, I actually went there in the flesh. I was going to save India! That was not a sinful ambition, but it was still wrong because I believed it was my ability and my effort that was going to do it. It is very easy as a Christian to offer your flesh to God as a "holy sacrifice." He doesn't want your literal flesh. He wants your flesh in surrendered submission to Him.

Only One Remedy for the Flesh: Kill It!

Scripture contains numerous examples of the flesh in action. One of the cases in point is from the scriptures about Esau. Esau was always independent. Even in the womb, Rebecca described that she could feel Esau and Jacob struggling. Esau came out red and hairy and was named from the primitive Hebrew root word *asah*, meaning "I do."

Esau is a picture of self-sufficient man. He was in many ways a nice guy. You would like him as a neighbor. You could borrow his lawnmower. He would help you build your garage. His house would always be in order. He was such a self-competent person that he felt he did not need God. He could go and hunt and provide his own dinner. He could look after himself, but he was not a religious person and did not feel any need for God.

Jacob, his brother, however, was a twisted character. He knew his need for God. In his twisted nature, Jacob sought after God. Esau simply didn't bother with God. The Bible calls Esau profane or godless. Profanity here simply means to be independent of God, of His nature, and of His life—simply being worldly. Godless would be another good description. Esau was a man without God.

In Esau, we find the kind of person who feels he is confident in himself. He has his life together. I can imagine him saying, "I can manage my life. I don't have any needs. I am the self-sufficient one. I don't need God. I don't need anybody. If I help you, then it's out of my own ability. I don't come to you for any need I have; I only come to you to be kind and helpful to you."

God said, "Jacob I loved, but Esau I hated" (Rom. 9:13). God loved Jacob because Jacob recognized he could not do anything for himself and desperately needed God. Esau had no use for God and therefore God had no relationship with him.

Esau gave birth to the tribe of Amalek, which waged war against the people of God. This was a constant battle in the Old Testament. Amalek serves as an allegorical picture of the battle of the flesh. Samuel brought King Saul the message from God that he should utterly destroy Amalek, saying, "Now go and attack Amalek and utterly destroy all that they have, and do not spare them" (1 Sam. 15). Saul went off and killed some of the Amalekites, but he allowed their king, Agag, to live along with the best of the sheep and the cattle. Do you remember for what purpose he kept them alive? The Bible says, "The soldiers took sheep and cattle from the plunder, the best of what was devoted to God, in order to sacrifice them to the LORD your God at Gilgal" (1 Sam. 15:21).

This is a picture of you and me saying, "Okay, I want to get rid of my bad temper. I want to stop smoking and not swear anymore. But since I am a very good musician, I will serve God with my musical ability." Yet you play your instrument in your natural ability and not in the Spirit. You can be a natural musician who is trying to serve God with natural flesh.

You can be a very good administrator, saying, "Okay, I'm going to get rid of all the wicked things, but I'm going to use this natural administrative gift of mine to serve God." If you think like this, you have a "King Agag" in your life, which you think does not need to die. However, that too must die! It is the very heart of the flesh. Those things that have a nice religious exterior and look good are the most dangerous.

We can try to salvage the best things of natural life and then offer them to God to serve Him in our own strength. But God says, "I don't want your flesh. I won't use any of your abilities and your gifts until you embrace the Cross, dying to yourself and your abilities." Then you will rise in Christ's resurrection power and use your gifts and abilities with God's power activating them.

Saul did not completely obey God. He destroyed 90–95 percent of the Amalekites but kept the best of them alive. Later on, we find Saul in yet another battle with the Philistines. The Philistines are a picture of the demonic, the Devil, and his forces, and Saul never got free from that warfare. He was a very courageous mighty man of God and he was always fighting God's enemies, but he never really dealt with the flesh. Finally,

Saul was sorely wounded in battle, when an Amalekite found him and thrust his spear into him and he died. If he had killed all of the Amalekites when God said so, this wouldn't have happened!

Three Dimensions of the Cross

I want you to see that this war with the flesh is serious. You have to destroy all that which is of the flesh before it kills you. You have to be serious about this.

Let us remind ourselves of the three ways in which the Cross works. First, the work of the Cross was the death of Jesus paying the penalty for our sins. Jesus died for me in a single act, once and for all. I do not have any part in it. I simply receive the benefit of Him dying on the Cross for me. This is His Cross.

The second work of the Cross was my dying with Christ in order that the old man might be put to death. This is also a once and for all single act. We are told very clearly in scripture that this work was completed and the verb is in the past perfect tense. It has already happened. My old man was crucified with Christ. This is our Cross.

And, finally, the third work of the Cross is a continuous life of denying ourselves in order to do the will of God. This is a continuous daily moment-by-moment dying to self. You have to take up your Cross daily, meaning you do not live for yourself, but for Him who died for you (2 Cor. 5:15). Furthermore, this is not His Cross. This is your Cross.

To understand this third dimension, we must understand Luke 9:23, where Jesus said, "If anyone would come after Me, let him deny himself and take up his Cross daily and follow Me."

To whom did Jesus say this? He said it to all of them, which includes you and me. Whose cross was it? It was their personal cross. There is a cross for each individual that follows Him! We cannot take up the cross upon which Jesus paid for our sins. We cannot take up the cross where Jesus put to death the old man once and for all. The only cross you must bear is the cross where you deny yourself and live exclusively for the purposes of God. This is your cross! You have to continuously pick it up on a daily, hour-by-hour, moment-by-moment basis for the rest of your life.

Jesus said that you cannot follow Him and be His disciple unless you take up your cross. The heart of this cross is that you deny yourself. We are dealing with your daily self-life. This is your flesh life. It requires a denial of yourself—what you think, what you feel, and what you want. It is the refusal to allow your soul and body to act independently of God and rule over you.

It might be a good idea to go to Africa and be a missionary, but if you do that on your own initiative, as your own decision, independent of God's direction, then that is the flesh. It might be good to go to the streets and evangelize, sing in the worship group, or play an instrument, but if you do these things of your own without asking or hearing from God, then that is the flesh operating. It is not God. Such efforts and acts do not bring life, only death.

We must be alerted to the activity of the flesh and recognize that if we are ever going to be free from the power of sin then we have to be free from the activity of the flesh. Very often, the flesh does not seem sinful. In fact, it can be trying desperately to do the will of God. It expends great effort in the attempt to do God's works. That's why this is so subtle.

Daily Crucifixion of the Flesh

After Jesus explained that those who would follow Him must deny themselves and take up their own personal cross (Luke 9:23), he goes on in Luke 14:25–27 to explain that "whoever does not bear his cross and come after Me cannot be My disciple." In these verses, Jesus is saying to each one of His disciples that to be His follower we have to each pick up our cross on a continuous daily basis.

This requires a daily, moment by moment, putting to death of the flesh life in order that sin might no longer have dominion over us. Paul describes the struggle in Romans 7:15–24, where he says in verse 15, "I do not understand, what I do. For what I want to do I do not do, but what I hate, I do. For I do not do the good I want to do, but the evil I do not want to do—this I keep on doing." He then cries out, "What a wretched man I am! Who will rescue me from this body that is subject to death?" (Rom. 7:19, 24), and declares his own answer, "Thanks be to God through Jesus Christ our Lord." Jesus Christ, and His Cross, is the answer!

If you read this passage in Romans 7:15–24 carefully, then you will find Paul uses the personal pronoun "I" about twenty-five times. This is what I have come to call spiritual "I-trouble." Many of us suffer from this "I-trouble," trying desperately by self-effort to do what only the Spirit of God can successfully do in us.

You have to hate the flesh the way God does. It gets square in the way of God's purpose and provides a platform in your life for sin to come and abide. Why is this? Galatians 5:17 explains, "For the flesh lusts against the Spirit, and the Spirit against the flesh; and these are contrary to one another, so that you do not do the things that you wish." So I say, live by the Spirit, and you will not gratify the desires of the flesh.

This is an irresistible law of the Spirit. The flesh and the Spirit are incompatible. In Romans 6:7, it says that sin finds opportunity through the flesh and by the flesh it enslaves us. This is the picture I want you to see. Weak flesh wants to do the will of God, but it can't. It is not blatantly wicked or rebellious like the old man. It is just weak. The religious flesh says, "I'll try and do the will of God! I will put forth my best effort!" but it always fails.

Striving after the flesh is sin's opportunity. It says in Romans 6 that sin finds its opportunity through the flesh and kills us. You have to see sin as the Bible portrays it. Sometimes sin seems to be personified and behaves like a cunning evil-being. There is no line here between demonic personalities and the flesh. They transition very easily from one to the other.

Every demon is a minister of a certain kind of sin. They often carry the name of the sin they specialize in. There is an unclean spirit, namely, the spirit of lust. There are demonic personalities that have specialized in a particular activity of sin. They seek to find an opportunity in a human being to influence them with the passion of their evil intent, which is the activity of that particular sin.

In Genesis 4, God warns Cain, when He says to him, "Cain! Sin is crouching at the door and its desire is for you." Sin is not described as an inanimate object but as an evil-being with a personality that was seeking to control him. Cain took offense at the dealings of God by becoming angry because his offering of self-effort was rejected. Then the sin, crouching at the door, took hold of him and possessed him.

You cannot draw the line between sin and the personality of the demon that perpetrates that sin. There is no line. If you play around with a sin then you are playing with a demon. If you persist in the sin, then you will eventually be controlled by the demon whether you are born again or not. The principle is the same.

If you are in the flesh, then you are a happy hunting ground for sin. A man in the flesh is unable to resist sin and does not have the power to resist the Devil. This has nothing to do with the old man.

This weakness is not because you are under the tyranny of the old man. The Cross, as we have already seen, has freed us from the old man. If Jesus had ever given place to His flesh, then He would have become vulnerable to sin. However, He never succumbed to the flesh, not even for one moment.

In the very beginning, Adam was innocently free from sin, but he only had to step out into independence to immediately know the power of sin taking control of his life. His first step was into independence, which led immediately to the second step into sin. Can you see that? That is why independence is so dangerous. God has freed you from the tyranny of the old man, but He does not remove the choice you always have to live in the flesh or in the Spirit. That is the choice you have to make for yourself. You have to make this decision many times every day.

Walk not after the Flesh but Walk in the Spirit

The alternative to the works of the flesh is walking in the Spirit. Galatians 5:1 explains, "Stand fast therefore in the liberty by which Christ has made us free, and do not be entangled again with a yoke of bondage." The freedom that Christ made possible for us does not mean we can now do whatever we like. Paul proceeds in Galatians 5:13 to explain, "For you, brethren, have been called to liberty; only do not *use* liberty as an opportunity for the flesh, but through love serve one another." And "If we live in the Spirit, let us also walk in the Spirit" (Gal. 5:25). Clearly, the way to avoid walking in the flesh is to walk in the Spirit. Walking in the Spirit is the only antidote for not fulfilling the lusts of the flesh.

This point is made over and over in Romans and Galatians. As we read in Galatians 5:16, "Walk in the Spirit, and you shall not fulfill the lust of the flesh." And then in Romans 8:1, it says, "There is therefore now no condemnation to those who are in Christ Jesus, who do not walk according to the flesh, but according to the Spirit." We read again in verse 4 "that the righteous requirement of the law might be fulfilled in us who do not walk according to the flesh but according to the Spirit." And finally, in Romans 5:2 we learn, "For the law of the Spirit of life in Christ Jesus has made me free from the law of sin and death."

However, before we can walk in the Spirit, we first have to learn how to not walk in the flesh. We have walked in the flesh for so many years that we do it instinctively without realizing it. If something happens unexpectedly, we react in a fleshly way before we even realize what we've done.

Scripture says again and again that sin finds its opportunity through the flesh and through the flesh it kills us. Sometimes people are struggling with sins, but what they should really be dealing with is the flesh, because the flesh is the door through which sin has entered to kill us. Inevitably, flesh will lead to sin. It is as certain as the pull of gravity.

The Law of Gravity

The pull of the law of sin and death through the flesh is so carefully spelled out for us in the book of Romans in chapters 6–8. It is relentless law, just like the law of gravity in its operation. Gravity takes no note of who you are, what time of day it is, what your nationality is, or what your geographical location is. None of these things matter. If you jump off a building at anytime, anywhere in the world, then you will accelerate toward the ground at a predictable speed. The pull of gravity is responsible for that. You can shout out whatever you like, "I don't believe in gravity! I don't believe in gravity!" but you will still go down toward the ground at the same speed.

It is interesting to study the history of aviation and see how men tried to conquer the law of gravity. Frenchmen, it seems, were the most desirous for this victory over gravity. There was something that made them desperate to learn how to fly; they tried all kinds of crazy things. All types of ingenious flying machines were invented, but the weakness of these inventions was that they all relied on the strength of the human arms to flap their man-made wings like a bird. One man even leaped off the Eiffel Tower in Paris, convinced he was going to fly, but you know what happened to him? He crashed to the ground and killed himself! They always relied on their own strength and self-effort.

The Law of Aerodynamics

It was not until man discovered a higher law, the first law of aerodynamics, that he identified the power to overcome gravity. Let me try to illustrate this for you. Take a piece of stiff paper and slightly curve it and then blow over the top surface of the paper. As you blow over the top surface, notice what happens; the paper begins to lift all by itself! "Lift" is possible because a partial vacuum is created on the underside of the paper by the current of air flowing over the top surface, and that is the principle by which all modern aircraft fly. Man began to learn to fly once he discovered the power of the wind!

If you get into a modern plane and it begins taxiing down the runway, it is exploiting the law of aerodynamics. When the plane reaches sufficient speed, it can rise up in the air and begin to fly and it does not even feel that gravity exists anymore. In fact, you feel like you have conquered gravity, but if you were to open the door of the plane and step out, you would soon discover that gravity is still there! While you are inside the plane, the power of the wind over the curved wings gives the plane this incredible lift so that it can fly. You are able to overcome the law of gravity as long as you stay in the plane and maintain the necessary speed.

The Spirit of Life in Christ Jesus

Spiritually, there is a law in the spirit realm called the "law of the Spirit of life in Christ Jesus." If your whole self is in Christ and remains in Him, then the power of the Spirit can carry you in such a way that the law of sin and death no longer has any pull over you. This only works while you are in Christ Jesus. If you step out of Christ Jesus and go back into your old self-life, you will immediately plummet back into sin's control. The law of sin and death will pull you down into the same old defeat that you experienced before.

The principle is very similar to flying and you must stay in Him to stay in victory! There is a power in God's grace through the Cross, which keeps us above the pull of things that previously pulled us down into sin and death.

If you are in Christ Jesus, then you cannot be in yourself. If you are in yourself, then you cannot be in Christ Jesus. Furthermore, there is nothing automatic about it. This is a daily moment-by-moment choosing of the way you want to live. There is no once and for all crisis here. It is a continual daily affair. There is no one who can lay hands on you to receive something that gives you permanent victory. There is no audio message or book you can buy that can give it to you once and for all. You have to live moment by moment in Christ Jesus. You must learn to live according to the law of the Spirit of life in Christ Jesus.

If you live that way, then you will find the power of sin broken in your life and you will be free from the law of sin and death because the law of sin and death only works in the flesh. The law of sin and death cannot work in Christ Jesus. The law of the Spirit of life works in Christ and the law of sin and death works in the flesh.

If you go from Christ back into the flesh, then you move from one law to the other. They are equally relentless and powerful and you can go from victory to failure in a fraction of time or vice versa. You will never ever get out of the bondage of the flesh until you come to live moment by moment in complete dependence upon the Lord Jesus Christ.

Live in the Spirit and Walk in the Spirit

We are also told in chapter 5 of Galatians that if we wish to walk in the Spirit then we must also live in the Spirit. In fact, if you do not live in the Spirit, then you cannot walk in the Spirit. Let me give you an illustration of this.

Some time ago I was in Hyderabad, India, a city and a country that I love and know very well. I lived in India for many years, and the Indian people became very precious to me. Today, however, I do not live in India. I live in America. As I write, I can picture in my mind the streets of Hyderabad or Mumbai. I can imagine myself going into a shop and buying things because I know these cities so well, but it is only in my mind. I cannot realize it in fact because I am not living there anymore.

In the same way, in your mind you can mentally want to be spiritual and make spiritual decisions. You can have a great desire to walk in the Spirit and overcome the flesh, but this will never happen until you are actually living in the Spirit. The place where you actually live is the only place where you can actually walk! If you live in the Spirit, then you can walk in the Spirit and do the works of the Spirit and the flesh will lose its power over you. If you only give mental assent to the Spirit and actually live in the flesh, then there is no way you can actually walk in the Spirit.

You must make certain choices regarding the way you want to live. You have to let the Spirit of God discipline you and bring you under His authority in every way. The Spirit of God does not like watching inappropriate television programs. He will refuse to watch them with you. The Spirit of God will not shout at your wife. He just does not do that sort of thing. The Spirit of God will not touch anything that is financially questionable. He will not continue to have fellowship with you if you cross that line. If you do not live God's way, He will not come and live in you your way. If you want to live in the Spirit, then as Peter said you must learn "to live in the Spirit like God" (1 Pet. 4:6).

The Spirit will draw you to Himself and teach you the way He lives so that you can actually live in the Spirit like Him. If you live in the Spirit, then you can walk in the Spirit just like Jesus did. The Bible clearly says that when you walk in the Spirit then you will not fulfill the lusts of the flesh. There is no cure, no special anointed bottle of oil, and no audio message that will deliver you from a life lived in the flesh. Instead, Jesus is offering you a life of continual self-crucifixion, which is the only thing that can accomplish living in the Spirit.

It is a life where you agree with God as to how wicked and unregenerate your flesh is and you come to hate the flesh the way God does. You must make the decision to agree with God that the only remedy for the flesh is to nail it to the Cross and kill it. The Bible says, "Those who are Christ's have crucified the flesh with its passions and desires" (Gal. 5:24). They have decided not to allow the flesh any room or expression in their life! Their flesh is such a wicked sinner that they will not allow it to live!

Finally, you get into Christ Jesus and learn to walk in the Spirit, which is a day-by-day, moment-by-moment learning experience. At first, you will find it is hard to stay in the Spirit continually. You walk in the Spirit for a little while and then slip back into fleshly ways. If this happens to you, then you must repent immediately and return to your place in Christ Jesus.

You will find that God will retrain your automatic reactions to people and to circumstances. The Father will reveal the fleshly nature of certain habits in your life until you learn how to go on continuously walking in the

Spirit and put these habits to death. You will find the power of the flesh gets weaker and weaker, causing sin to lose its hold over your life.

You will also find that everything the Bible says is true. You can live a life where you are not in bondage to anything. I would not dream of trying to boast in myself, but I will testify to the power of God in my life. I have found this word to be true. I am not teaching you theory but the practice of my own life. If it were not true then, I would not teach it to you. If it works for me, then it will certainly work for you.

What I am saying to you is practical, but you have to make certain decisions. You have to decide to take the flesh as seriously as God does and agree with God that the flesh is only fit for execution upon the Cross. You have to agree with God that not even the best of the Amalekites shall live. They all have to die.

You also have to agree that God can take the sword of the Spirit and execute every manifestation of the flesh in your life. You will not complain but you will rejoice with God while it is happening. You will let the Spirit of God train you how to live in the Spirit more completely. You will see the law of the Spirit of life in Christ Jesus operating in your life and constantly overcoming the law of sin and death.

You must decide you will not accept any substandard level of living until this has become a practical and realized experience in your life. When the flesh is exposed, you must be as ruthless against it as God is. You must hate it as much as He hates it.

If you will receive this, then you can come into a life of power and victory, which will cause the Spirit of God to flow through you without hindrance. You will be blessed; you will be a blessing to many people and a continual terror and frustration to the Devil. You will also know that every victory and all the success was not your doing but that of the Spirit of God working in you. If anything glorious has happened in my life, then it is because the Spirit of God has had the freedom to act through my life. So all the glory belongs to Him, and none of it is mine. That can be as true for you as it is for me!

CHAPTER 7

THE POWER OF THE CROSS TO OVERCOME THE WORLD

But God forbid that I should boast except in the Cross of our Lord Jesus Christ, by whom the world has been crucified to me, and I to the world. (Gal. 6:14)

Notice the words in Galatians 6:14. It is vital that we see how the influence of the world is overcome by the power of the Cross. Paul said, "But God forbid that I should boast except in the Cross of our Lord Jesus Christ, by whom the world has been crucified to me, and I to the world." Note the double crucifixion mentioned here. There is a power in the Cross to crucify the world to us and also power in the Cross to crucify us to the world.

In spite of what the Bible clearly says about the dangers of friendship with the world and sympathetic attitudes to the world system, the majority of Christians are in bondage to this world to varying degrees. Many love the world and even nurture an appetite for the things of the world. Others simply succumb to the pressure of the worldly system surrounding them. They just give in, saying, "I can't resist the pressure of the world. It's too strong for me." They go to their jobs Monday morning intending to be a great witness for Christ, but instead they cave in and find themselves behaving just like everybody else. Unfortunately, this is the experience of too many Christians.

I want you to understand that the amazing Cross has tremendous power to break the pull of the world in our lives and is the answer we need. We are strongly exhorted in scripture, "Do not love the world or the things in the world" (1 John 2:15). John goes on to say, "If anyone loves the world, the love of the Father is not in him. For all that is in the world—the lust of the flesh, the lust of the eyes and the pride of life—is not of the Father but is of the world" (1 John 2:16). By the power of the Cross, we can be delivered from the world. Deliverance from the world means the following:

- We do not think like the world.
- We do not accept the standards of the world.
- We are not in bondage to the fears and anxieties of the world.
- We do not need the comforts, luxuries, or securities of the world.
- We do not have longing desires or appetites for the things of this world.

The world in 1 John describes a demonically controlled system with an atmosphere that is suffocating. Our only place of safety is in Christ and the power of the Cross. We are living in a time where everything is increasingly being shaken, including world economics, but in Christ we can have complete peace when everything is shaking around us. Remember how the children of Israel fared when God was judging Egypt. In Goshen, where the Hebrew people lived, the economy went on booming and they didn't suffer like the Egyptians (see Gen. 47: 1–27; Ex. 8:1–32, 9:1–35). Can you believe God for a Goshen experience in these days for yourself, your ministry, your business and for your church?

It seems, at this time, that there is not a nation in the world that is not in upheaval. Surely, it's a fulfillment of God's promise where He said, "Once more I will shake all heaven and earth, the sea and dry land; and I will shake all nations" (Hag. 2:6–7; Heb. 12:26).

This shaking frightens those who do not know Christ. However, those who know Him should never be shaken. The times of trouble are the beginning of God's answer and the fulfillment of His promise that He would pour out His glory on the face of the whole earth. To do this, God must free us from our own idols! People must be free from the world's idols before they really have an open heart to receive the Lord Jesus Christ.

The anarchy in the Middle East and conflict in Syria, Iraq, Iran, and Northern Africa and even the rest of the world is to be expected. But, also, as a result of this shaking, thousands are receiving Jesus Christ around the world. Every shaking in the world has a divine purpose in it. There should not be anxiety in our hearts.

In the first eleven chapters of Romans, Paul sets forth some important theological truths and explains the great cosmic purposes of God for both Jew and Gentile. While we strive to grasp these theological truths, the most important thing is to live what you now know. Beginning in Romans 12:1, Paul sets out what must be our right and practical response to these truths—presenting ourselves to God.

The Proper Use of Our Body

Scripture is clear about the way we should conduct our lives. In Romans 12:1, we are instructed to offer our "bodies as living sacrifices, holy, acceptable to God, which is your reasonable service." Let me ask you a simple question: Have you done this? Can you say, "Lord, my body is available to You for Your use just as the Body of Jesus Christ was available to the Father and the Spirit during His thirty-three and a half years upon the earth."

In Psalm 40 and Hebrews 10, the Spirit of Christ was anticipating the day when He would receive a body. He cries out in Hebrews 10:5, "But a body You have prepared for Me." Then He continues in Hebrews 10:7, "I have come…to do Your will, O God." There is only one legitimate use for our body, which is to do the will of God.

When I became a Christian many years ago, this was so obvious to me. I even understood this before I was converted. If there was a living God, who had created me, then He had the right as the Creator to rule over my life. He has every right to do what He wants with my life. By the grace of God, I have sought to put this truth into practice ever since. Have you done that? Can you say, "Oh Lord, to the best of my ability I have given my body to You as a living sacrifice? I will go anywhere, live anywhere, do anything that You choose to do through my body?"

This is a simple yet very deep commitment to Jesus Christ. That is what we are being asked to do here. Have you done it? Or will you decide to do this now?

Forsaking the World's Standards, Rewards, and Thinking

Romans 12:2 continues instructing in how we must live, saying, "do not be conformed to this world, but be transformed by the renewing of your mind, that you may prove what is that good and acceptable and perfect will of God."

After we have settled the question of the proper use of our body, we must then go on to experience a renewal in the way we think. I would like to quote the paraphrase translation by J. B. Philips of the first part of this same verse because he brings out an important truth very clearly. He writes, "Don't let the world squeeze you into its own mold but be transformed by the renewing of you mind."

The world has the capacity to exert tremendous pressure on people's lives and especially the way they think. Unconsciously, people are shaped by the media and by all the years of our secular education to think and act in certain culturally acceptable or politically correct ways. Deliverance from this secular or humanist world view begins with a radical change of thinking. We must have a totally renewed mind so that we do not think in this worldly way anymore, but rather have a biblical world view.

I am not talking about the obvious sins of immorality, lust, and greed, but the subtler ways in which the world influences our thinking. For example, many people find their security in material things. Their life consists in the abundance of what they own. Others believe that in order to be successful and important they must climb the career ladder in their profession. The more people they supervise, the more important and secure they feel.

Sometimes people are even promoted beyond their real level of competence. This is called the Peter Principle. They finally are promoted to a position where they cannot comfortably handle the job because it has become too big for them. And rather than security and prestige, they spend the rest of their career clinging to a job that is too big for them while pushing down everyone who is trying to steal it away from them. They live in a state of competitive insecurity while eating their hearts out at night in anxiety. It would be unthinkable in the world's eyes to go to your boss and say, "Sir, this job is too big for me. I would rather go down a couple of steps to a job I can handle without anxiety." If you did that, then you would probably be fired for lack of initiative and drive.

That is worldly thinking. Do not let the world squeeze you into its mold. Be renewed in the spirit of your mind. Do you know what success is in God's sight? Total success in God's sight is doing what you were created to do in the way God created you to do it!

According to Psalm 139, each one of us was handmade by God. David literally says, "You stitched me (or wove me together or formed me) in my mother's womb." There never was any other person just like you and there never will be anybody like you again. You are not an accident. It does not matter whether your parents planned you or not. God planned you and created you for His pleasure and purpose. The psalmist cried out, "For You formed my inward parts; You covered me in my mother's womb. I will praise You, for I am fearfully *and* wonderfully made. Marvelous are Your works, and *that* my soul knows very well" (Ps. 139:13–14).

God wrote all your days before you were even born. We are told in Psalm 139:16 that God recorded all your days before there was a single one of them. God planned you and put together a particular blend of characteristics and personality and made you the unique person who you are. He was well satisfied with what He did. He did not make a mistake. He did it perfectly.

The only thing wrong with you is that God's perfect handiwork has been marred by sin. When you get rid of the sinful nature, then what is left is pure gold. Every one of us is rich beyond measure in the gold of God's creative handiwork. You are beautiful. You are perfect. You are fearfully and wonderfully made. You are exactly right for what He intends you to do in this life and for what you are supposed to be in eternity. Do you believe that?

Have you come to the place where you really like yourself? Have you ever said to God, "Father, you did a good job when you made me?" I know when I came to this liberating realization. I finally came to the place where I liked me. Apart from the aberration of sin, which God has gloriously dealt with in the Cross, I am fearfully and wonderfully made. I am so happy to be me.

It is also important to understand that God has cut a furrow for you in His eternal purpose. It says in Psalm 139 and also in Ephesians 2:10 that God has prepared good works for us to do. Before God made the world, He planned a path for your life. He made something for you to do that only you can do in His eternal purpose. Now isn't that exciting?

Real success occurs when your unique personality and character is dropped into the perfect slot that God has cut for you in His eternal purposes in this world. When you drop into that slot and you start walking in the purposes of God, only then are you truly successful. You cannot be more successful than when you are doing God's will. If you miss God's will, you miss the offer of a successful life. Success has nothing to do with the fame of your name, the size of your bank account, or the initials after your name. These things have no value in the sight of God.

Real fulfillment and success is discovering and working God's purpose for your life. Doing God's will in this way also carries the maximum eternal reward. You are going to be rewarded in eternity for your faithfulness in doing God's will in this life and not at all for your own self-generated prominence and success. This is totally different from how the world thinks and behaves. The Kingdom of God thinks the opposite way to the world. According to Jesus, if you want to be the greatest in the Kingdom, then you must become the servant of everybody. If you want to be powerful, then you become meek. If you desire to serve Jesus, then you must become truly humble like Him.

This sounds crazy, but this is what Jesus said. Am I not quoting scripture to you? Can you see how we have to start thinking in an entirely different way? We may pay lip service to these truths, but in actual fact, many Christians are still practicing worldly thinking. We still want to be someone in terms of worldly standards. Even in the church, we can think worldly and believe we have to have a visible position in the church to have any value. When you are in God's will, you have your greatest value. Everybody in God's Kingdom is equally valuable, but they just have different functions.

A deacon who carefully puts the chairs out and wipes them down and prays over each chair, saying, "God bless the person who sits here" is just as important as the person who stands behind the pulpit to preach the Word. If a person does what God has called him to do faithfully, he will receive the same reward in eternity as a world-famous apostle. An apostle has to be faithful in his apostolic calling just as a deacon must be faithful in his serving. If each one is faithful, then each receives the same reward. Do you believe that? It is better to be a faithful deacon than an unfaithful apostle.

The Bible also warns that teachers are going to be judged with a greater standard of severity than others (James 3:1). Everyone whom God calls, He also equips. Everyone He equips, He expects a good return on His investment. Jesus said, "to whom much is given, from him much will be required" (Luke 12:48). Have you come to this way of thinking?

For most people, their life is approximately fifty to eighty years. Compared with eternity, this life is like the blink of an eye. Now who would want to invest everything in the blink of an eye and miss being in the right place doing the right thing for all eternity? Anyone must be crazy to think that way. Yet most of the world thinks that way. The large majority does not view life in the light of eternity.

Essential Steps into Freedom from the World

As I discussed in chapter one, there has to be a renewing of our minds to forsake the world's standards, rewards, and thinking. We have to come to what philosophers call "thesis and antithesis thinking." You become clear thinkers like God. If one thing is true, then its opposite is false. If one thing is right, then its opposite is wrong. In other words, the God we serve is a clear black and white or right and wrong God. Some things are eternally right or righteous, and other things are eternally wrong and unrighteous. God never changes His mind.

Scriptures teach every married man should live with his wife in holy marriage until death and have no intimate relationships with any other women. If that is right, then any other intimate relationship with another woman is wrong. This is plain and simple. Yet some Christian people think they can play with fire and not get burned. God does not change. His simple black-and-white standards are meant to protect us from harm. It is sin that harms us, not God. God would not keep any good thing from us. If God forbids something, it is because it is harmful to us. There is a great need to become childlike in thinking. I came from a scientific background and I was an agnostic. My Christian grandmother prayed for my salvation, and God used a couple of Mormon missionaries who "accidentally" introduced me to Jesus. The God we serve is big! See Appendix I.

So I know two things are absolutely true. First of all, anybody can be saved! If you had seen me when I was twenty-seven years of age as an arrogant young man, no one would have believed that I could ever turn to Jesus Christ, but God made it happen. Hallelujah! I know the power of God's written Word to renew the mind. When I was steeped in arrogant intellectualism, the grace of God brought me to a childlike trust in the Bible as the Word of the living God. I believe that every word of the Bible is inspired by God and is without error. I have built my life on that standard. I have lived this way for over fifty years. I have stepped out into all kinds of scary situations trusting in His Word alone. God has repeatedly proved His faithfulness. Faith requires us to step out trusting the Word of God alone to fully prove the reality of God.

I speak with absolute conviction, and I thank God for changing my whole way of thinking. I was ruthlessly ambitious to get to the top of my profession, but actually I would have become an utter failure in terms of eternal value.

Are you free from this worldly thinking? Have you been renewed in the spirit of your mind so as to think like God? Do you have the same simple black-and-white approach to life that God has? God said, "For My thoughts are not your thoughts, nor are your ways My ways" (Isa. 55:8). Jesus said, " For what profit is it to a man if he gains the whole world, but loses his own soul?" (Matt.16:26).

The Spirit of God is prepared to teach you how to think like God. This is a tremendous privilege. You can increasingly learn how to change your thinking and to judge things from a truly godly perspective. What a gracious God we serve.

Steps into Freedom from the World

At the beginning of this chapter, I discussed what we must do to be delivered from worldly thinking and behavior. Devoting your body to God and renewing your mind are the beginning of this deliverance. However, in addition, for complete deliverance of worldly ways, believers must also accomplish overcoming the lust of the eyes, the lust of the flesh, and the pride of life. John describes this in his First Letter of John 2:15–17:

> Do not love the world or the things in the world. If anyone loves the world, the love of the Father is not in him. For all that is in the

world, the lust of the flesh, the lust of the eyes and the pride of life is not of the father but is of the world and the world is passing away and the lust of it, but he, who does the will of God abides forever.

And James 4:4 says that "friendship with the world is enmity with God." You cannot love God and the world simultaneously. You will love one and hate the other.

And in Matthew 6:24, Jesus says. "No one can serve two masters; for either he will hate the one and love the other, or else he will be loyal to the one and despise the other. You cannot serve God and mammon." Some of these scriptures we know, but do we really believe them for ourselves? Do we apply them to our lives?

You cannot serve God and mammon. You cannot serve God and riches. You have to choose. Are you going to go for the things of this world or for God? It is impossible to serve both. It is important to think about this and understand it because Jesus says in Matthew 19:23–24:

Assuredly, I say to you that it is hard for a rich man to enter the kingdom of heaven. And again I say to you, it is easier for a camel to go through the eye of a needle than for a rich man to enter the kingdom of God.

In other words, the passion to become rich means that you will almost certainly miss the Kingdom of God. That is what Jesus is saying. There are some wonderful exceptions, but most rich men and women never enter the kingdom. Money is not necessarily evil, but the Bible emphatically says that "the love of money is the root of all evil" (1 Tim. 6:10).

Suppose someone says to you, "I'm going to give you twenty million dollars just for your own enjoyment," but you discover that there are some unrighteous conditions. Would you say, "Absolutely not! I would hate to miss the Kingdom simply to get twenty million dollars to spend on myself"?

I am serious. I would like us to get honest with God, and I intend to be so myself. If a check landed on my desk for $20 million, then what would I really do? I would certainly be very fearful and would want to make sure it was from God and then see it was used righteously for God's Kingdom's purposes. It is a historic fact that most who win lotteries become ruined in a short period of time. They are completely unable to cope with the traps and bondages that come with vast amounts of money.

I do not want to miss God's Kingdom. If Jesus said that almost every rich man is going to miss the Kingdom, then I had better listen and clarify my attitude toward money and riches. The person who becomes rich is often captivated by his riches, not by God.

On the other hand, the Bible does promise that there is financial sufficiency for all believers. They will also prosper for the purpose of being great givers. There is no blessedness in being poor. As I have said, excessive riches can be very dangerous, but it is even more dangerous to covet riches whether you are poor or have plenty. It may surprise you that this demonic heart attitude can possess the poor as well as the wealthy. Are you free from that heart attitude?

I have met many in India living in very poor circumstances on approximately $300 a year and, in contrast, the extravagantly wealthy. In either case, whether extreme poverty or extravagant wealth, it is impossible to enter the Kingdom of God when the heart is bound with greed and love of money and material possessions. What would you do if you suddenly found there was the prospect of your earning significantly more? How would you handle it? Would you say, "Fantastic! This is the most awesome thing that has happened to me in my life?" Then you would consider, "I have to be very prayerful how I handle this wealth." Even legitimate riches could cause us to miss the Kingdom. Love the Kingdom more than your money.

We have to be free from the love of money and the love of this world. What we do with what we have now will test our hearts.

On the other hand, the Bible promises that all those who obey God's principles will have sufficiency. Specifically, they will have sufficiency for every good work and all the legitimate necessities of life will be lovingly met by their Heavenly Father. In addition to that, they will have abundance to give away for every good work. In other words, if God finds He can trust us to handle money righteously without getting snared by it, we are going to have plenty to give away. The only point in being a millionaire in the Kingdom is to have 90 percent of your income available to give away. If you are a millionaire, then you should be able to live easily on 10 percent of your income while giving 90 percent away. That is the only kind of Kingdom-millionaire that is really useful to God. Any other kind of millionaire can be destroyed by his riches.

In Hebrews 11:24, we see a man who made an important decision. "By faith Moses, when he became of age, refused to be called the son of Pharaoh's daughter." Why did Moses do this? If he had chosen to be called the son of the Pharaoh's daughter, then he would have guaranteed himself a high income and a permanent position of power and influence in the great Egyptian Empire. But he chose "rather to suffer affliction with the people of God than to enjoy the passing pleasures of sin, esteeming the reproach of Christ greater riches than the treasures in Egypt" (Heb. 11:25–26).

In other words, Moses was really looking at eternal things with a true perspective. He could have said, "If I am known as the son of the Pharaoh's daughter, I will receive all the riches of Egypt along with a powerful position in that kingdom for forty or fifty years. What is that compared with the treasure of Christ?" Moses made a sound business decision. "I would rather be rich in eternity and poor on earth! Plus, no moth can come and corrupt these riches. No thief can come and steal them and no enemy can possess it!"

Seeing Things from the Perspective of Eternity

If you can see eternal things and the Kingdom of God is real to you, then like Moses you can see that this is the only sensible decision. I am really concentrating on this because we have to look at our hearts. If we are occupied with earthly and material things, then our availability for the Kingdom is greatly reduced.

Eileen and I made an important decision for our family back in 1962. Even today, we are still living out the consequences of that decision. I had only been converted for about four years. I was doing my best scientific research work at the time with the Holy Spirit's help. I was the main inventor of a new product that Kodak marketed successfully for a number of years. My popularity and importance in the company was rising quickly when God suddenly called us to leave everything and go to India as missionaries.

The chairman of the board of Kodak and his legal adviser called me to London. They took me to lunch and spent the whole afternoon trying to persuade me to stay with the company. I said, "Look, I've just met the living God, and He has told me and my wife to go to India." I told them all about Jesus and my encounter with Him and how real He now was to me. At the end of our discussion, these men were fascinated with what they had heard. I had really talked sense to them; it became their problem. Then they said, "To be honest there are a dozen people eagerly waiting to step into our shoes." Their lives were empty of any eternal reality, and they would never take such a step themselves.

We moved to India without any financial support. We were moving simply trusting in the living God and His Word. Only God was going to supply our needs and the needs of our small family. I explained this plainly and simply.

I learned, years later, that the chairman of the Board in England had immediately contacted the general manager of Kodak India in Bombay and urged him to make contact with me and keep in touch with Kodak UK. He said, "If Alan Vincent looks hungry or needy and looks like he wants to return to England, then you have my authority to fly him and his whole family back to England at our expense. We will put him back into the research laboratory where he belongs. You tell him, 'Right, you've had your religious adventure. Now go back to England and get on with the good work that you were doing so well.'"

When I came back to England after my first four years of service in India, I was again invited to a meeting with representatives of Kodak. I was told, "I'm glad you are back in England. We have a wonderful new opportunity for you." I was taken to see a completely new laboratory. The Kodak representative said, "We need you as the team leader. You can have charge of the whole thing." Then some of the men who used to work for me took me out to lunch in their wonderful new cars and entertained me in their lovely new homes. The Devil said to me, "You fool! Look at what you have given up. Don't you see what you could have become?" For a little while, I toyed with the idea of taking the job and I wobbled in my resolution to go back to India.

I have to confess that I thought I was free, but when I started to feel the attraction of these worldly things again, I was almost pulled back again into the world. A few days later, I went to a local church meeting. It was not a very good meeting, but somehow God got through to me there. I fell on my knees and repented and said, "Father, I almost lost my eternal reward. I almost made the biggest mistake of my life. Please forgive me." I immediately wrote to the chairman of the Board and said, "I am sorry to inform you that I cannot accept your kind invitation. I am returning to India as a missionary." Bombay, India, then became our home for the next decade or more.

I came very near to making the biggest mistake of my life. Believe me when I say that I know how strong the pull of this world can be. I did not go to India as a missionary because I was a failure in other things. In the eyes of the world, I was a big success when Jesus interrupted my career and called me to leave everything and follow Him.

I am looking back now after about fifty years of ministry. I am moving closer to the day when I will stand before the Lord and give an account of my life. Many of my lifelong friends have passed into glory, men and women whom I knew loved and served God for years. It is becoming more and more attractive to depart and be with the Lord in glory. I don't know how much longer I will live before I join them, but I want every moment to count for His Kingdom!

I sometimes think, *Oh, I thank God I made the right decisions in those ambitious years of my twenties and early thirties*. If you have a tremendous driving force to be something or someone, then direct that force to Jesus and to the Kingdom of God. Be successful in the Kingdom. Be on fire for God. Use all you have for Jesus. Make a mark for God. Do not let the world squeeze you into its own mold. You have to make a decision. Moses made a choice and it was the right one. You also have to make a choice!

Seek First His Kingdom

In Matthew 6:33, Jesus said, "But seek first the kingdom of God and His righteousness, and all these things shall be added to you." Maybe you know this verse by heart. The Greek word for "seek" is *zeteo*. It is very strong. Just before making this statement, Jesus had talked about hungry people seeking food. Have you ever been desperately hungry? Most of us have never experienced real hunger.

Have you ever been really thirsty? I remember driving across India on one occasion. We drove all day across a barren area, and I had made a big mistake regarding the amount of water we needed to take with us. It was a sweltering hot day. We were miles from civilization. The car had no air conditioning. We could only drive with the windows open, allowing some air to circulate. We were drinking water constantly.

Starting at 4:30 a.m., we had to complete 420 miles across these difficult desert roads in order to reach our destination by 9:00 p.m. for the night. By about 3:00 p.m., our water had run out. We drove the rest of the day without water. I cannot describe to you how thirsty I felt when we finally reached our lodging for the night. My host came out to greet me, but I blurted out rather rudely, "Where is the water? I must have some water quickly!" I did not say, "How nice to see you! How charming your house is." I desperately wanted that water immediately.

He said, "Oh, oh, I'll get some water for you," and he ran and got it. I must have drunk half a gallon of water in less than a minute.

Then I said, "Oh, that feels so much better. Excuse me! I was so thirsty I just couldn't think of anything else." Courtesy and politeness went out of the window.

That is the strength of this Greek word *zeteo* when it says "seek first the Kingdom of God." It is like a hungry man desperately going for food. It is like a thirsty man desperately going for water. Make sure the Kingdom is first in your life. Seek first the Kingdom of God and His righteousness and then all these other things will be yours as well.

If you do this, you can have a lot of fun in the world, but the world can never put its shackles on you. It can never get hold of you because you are a free man. It cannot force you to do anything or to go anywhere against God's will. It cannot buy you and it cannot bribe you or corrupt you. You are free from the world because you have made certain choices.

You become a free man to do the will of God. The amazing thing is that when you become that free God allows a new anointing and a new authority to come upon you. You end up being more successful in the Kingdom than you ever could have been in the world. You actually have all you need as a by-product of seeking God and His Kingdom first!

Loving the World Like God

Our first decision must be to forsake the wrong love of this world. The word "world" is used here to mean the world system that operates in defiance of God and His role as King and Lord. When God says, "Don't love the world," how can He also say at the same time that we should love the world as He does in John 3:16? "For God so loved the world that He gave His only begotten Son, that whosoever believes in Him should not perish but have everlasting life."

The answer is that God loves the world redemptively, but He has no affection for its ways or its standards. We have to be in the world and love it in the same redemptive way for the sake of those for whom Christ gave His life to save them. But the world's system, its values, and ways are in direct conflict with God, and in that sense, we have to hate the world. I hate the world system. The more I touch it, the more corrupt and hollow it seems. At the same time, I have a yearning to see the whole world saved and transformed. If I knew it to be God's will, I would gladly live in India for the rest of my life. I would lay my life down for the precious people of that country, even with its pockets of corruption, darkness, wickedness, deception, and evil.

I have seen in certain parts of the world that there is a vileness about a society that has never been touched by the Gospel of Christ. You cannot appreciate what we have had in the Western Christianized nations until you travel and live in countries such as India, Communist nations, China, or many of the nations of Africa and the Middle East. The world without Christ, including our western nations, is horrible. It is evil. It is violent. It is corrupt. Yet we should love the world redemptively, like God.

Embrace the Double Crucifixion

The next step in finding freedom from the world is embracing the dual crucifixion of ourselves to the world and the world to us. Galatians 6:14 is very important to understand: "But God forbid that I should ever boast except in the Cross of our Lord Jesus Christ, by whom the world has been crucified to me, and I to the world." As I mentioned earlier in this chapter, there are two crucifixions described here. The first crucifixion is that the world has been crucified to me. The second crucifixion is that I have been crucified to the world. What does this mean?

First of all, Kingdom believers live as people who have seen through the world and all its deceptive attractions. As a result, we want none of it. The only reason that we stay in the world is to see the Kingdom of God established and advanced through our lives and activity. We come in direct opposition to the workers of darkness, for example, porn operators, drug lords, and moneymaking racketeers; they experience the power of the Kingdom of God invading their society. They will often say, "Let's get rid of these Christian do-gooders. They are ruining our business."

When the collision of two kingdoms occurs, there are those who will lay down their lives for the Gospel. This is increasingly happening already in many parts of the world. Recently, Christians in Iraq and dozens of other places were persecuted and summarily assassinated because of their belief in Christ. Christians in the Indian state of Andhra Pradesh were killed by Hindu militants. This tragedy did not make the headline news. A whole company of believers meeting together were massacred by Hindu fanatics because they were destroying the kingdom of darkness with their lives and their prayers. God is beginning to break into the dark regions and strongholds of the enemy. The day will come when the Devil has to pay for his wicked counterattacks if we keep our faith. I accept this double crucifixion. The world is crucified to me and I am crucified to the world; therefore, it should not be a surprise when the world system hates me. The world may want to crucify me the way they did Jesus. If necessary, I am prepared to pay that price because I so want the Kingdom to come. There is now a mutual enmity between the world, the Kingdom, and we who advance the Kingdom.

There must be a double crucifixion in order to have a faith that can overcome the world. While it may seem like it, the world system is not in charge. The pressure of this world is great; it can almost crush us at times, particularly, if we go against the world by seeking to bring in the Kingdom. At times, it seems that the world system has such a strong hold on the minds and hearts of men that it is impossible to change. But watch! We serve an everlasting Kingdom.

Think of the battle going on over abortion rights in many countries at this present time. Many Christians may doubt if the Church can ever turn it around. It seems to be so strong. However, in fact, the power of the Cross has already broken the power of the Devil! The power of the Cross is much stronger than all the powers of this world and much greater than the prince of this world.

The Ruler of This World Has Been Judged

Through the Cross, the ruler of this world has already been judged and cast down. In John 12:27–28, as Jesus is about to face the Cross, He says:

Now my heart is troubled, and what shall I say? Father, save me from this hour? But for this purpose I came to this hour. "Father, glorify your name." Then a voice came from heaven, I have glorified it, and will glorify it again.

Jesus continued in verses 30–33:

This voice was for your benefit, not mine. Now is the time for judgment on this world; now the prince of this world will be driven out. And I, when I am lifted up from the earth, will draw all people to myself. He said this to show the kind of death he was going to die.

At the Cross, the Devil, the prince of this world, was judged and cast down!

Then in John 16:7, Jesus is explaining to His disciples that His going away was going to be a good thing for them: "Nevertheless I tell you the truth. It is to your advantage that I go away; for if I do not go away, the Helper (Greek: Paracletos) will not come to you; but if I depart, I will send Him to you." Jesus was really asking them, "Do you believe it is better for Me to go away so that the Holy Spirit can come and actually live right inside each one of you rather than just have Me physically present with you; in which case you can only watch the Spirit working through Me? Which is honestly better?"

Which would you rather have today in your particular situation? Do you want the Holy Spirit to actually take complete possession of your humanity and then through you do even greater works than the works that Jesus did as He promised in John 14:12? Or do you want Jesus to physically walk the streets in your town while you just watch and admire Him?

Jesus then showed the that it was much better for Him to go away, to seal the covenant with His blood in heaven and so complete the total triumph of Calvary, and then return in the power of the resurrection to indwell them by His Holy Spirit. Jesus said that it was much better for the Holy Spirit to come. While Jesus was on earth, He could only physically be in one place at a time. Although the fullness of the Godhead was dwelling in His humanity, there was such restriction on how much He could accomplish. But after Pentecost when the Holy Spirit came to them all, Jesus greatly increased the power of His works through them and simultaneously worked through a multitude of His servants in many different places at the same time. Hallelujah!

When He Comes to You

In John 16:7, the phrase "comes to you" needs some careful explanation, which is not clear in most English translations. What Jesus is actually saying is that the Holy Spirit will no longer just be with them but will actually come to them, and on the Day of Pentecost, He will enter into them spiritually and dwell within them.

How is the Holy Spirit going to come and convict the world of sin and of righteousness and judgment? He will do it by coming to you! He is not going to float in the atmosphere like a cloud of glory over your city or country. He must come to His saints, to His people on earth, and then do His works through them. He moves through people.

Notice what the Holy Spirit will do when He comes.

> *He will convict the world of sin and righteousness and judgment: of sin, because they do not believe in Me; of righteousness, because I go to My Father and you see Me no more; of judgment, because the ruler of this world is judged.* (John 16:8–11)

For the world to be convinced of sin, the Holy Spirit needs to come to you and through your words and your works convince the world. Also, the world will see that the prince of this world has already been judged by the public casting out his demon spirits with just a word from you. This is going to happen when the Spirit comes to you.

We are told in John's Gospel that the Holy Spirit will come to us, but He is also a great fighter. He is a fighter when it comes to the Devil. How did Jesus cast out demons? He cast them out with a word from the Spirit of God (Matt. 12:28). Once Jesus was anointed with the Holy Spirit and power, He began an aggressive almighty assault upon the kingdom of darkness. It was the Holy Spirit clothed in the humanity of Jesus that was launching that attack. He is the strong one that can break open the prison doors and let the captives go free. If you make your humanity available to the Triune God as completely as Jesus did to the Holy Spirit and the Father, then the Holy Spirit can do as much through you as He did through Jesus. Do you believe that?

I believe that is why in parts of India today we are seeing a mighty breakthrough. These new Christians simply believe that the Spirit can move as much through them as He did through Jesus. When great demons rise up in anger and fury against them, they know that the One in them is greater than the demon confronting them. They know that every demon has to bow their knee to Jesus because He settled that issue at Calvary. That is where the prince of this world was judged and cast down. Legally, it was all settled at Calvary.

At the Cross the man Christ Jesus, recovered all that the First Adam had lost. Jesus, the Last Adam, legally recovered the rulership of the world that Adam had lost through his disobedience. Jesus won the court order at the Cross. He now has all power and all authority upon Earth and in Heaven.

Any claim by Satan to have control of any part of this world is totally illegal and untrue. Jesus was given a mandate and authority in His resurrection to throw the Devil out wherever He finds him. Satan still tries to cling to his illegal possessions. Therefore, he must be forcefully removed.

Enforcing Christ's Legal Right to Rule the World

The legality of world ownership was settled at Calvary, where Satan and his hordes of demons were totally defeated. However, Christ's victory requires human law-enforcement officers to make sure that the legal verdict of

Calvary is enforced upon earth. These "Kingdom-enforcement officers" must be empowered for their task, casting out demons and advancing the power of the Kingdom of God. Therefore, they must be anointed with all the power of the Holy Spirit.

To personalize this, you and I must believe that the Holy Spirit is able to be just as powerful in us and through us as He was in the humanity of Jesus.

This is totally true and I believe it. When I moved into the demon-infested, dark strongholds in India, I saw the power of God work through my humanity to do amazing miracles. I was amazed at what He did through a little nobody like me! Believe me, God can use anyone. He just needs their willingly surrendered humanity because it is God the Holy Spirit that does the works through His believers.

When we come to this place of faith, then He will start to work through us the way He worked through Jesus. In this way, He will convince the world that the prince of this world has already been judged. By demonstration, He will show the impotence of these demons as they try to hang on to their illegal possessions. The world will see them being cast out and the fear of Lord Jesus Christ, the only true God, will come upon them.

I have seen these things happen with my own eyes in villages throughout India and in various nations in Africa, the Americas, and Europe. I believe the day will come when some of you will be doing these things too.

There will be visible showdowns with the demonic powers. When these confrontations happen, don't be scared. Just know that the Holy Spirit has fought the greatest demons in the world and He has defeated them every time. It is impossible for God's Spirit to ever be defeated. Whenever Jesus and a demon met, the outcome was always the same: Jesus triumphed and the demon left defeated!

We once went into a particular village in India where there was strong idol worship. The whole village was demonized and controlled by the demons through some so-called Hindu holy men. These men were so sure of themselves and of their superior power that they publicly challenged us and said, "If your Jesus is so strong, then let us see what He can do."

They brought a raving, demon-possessed girl in chains to the door of this room where John Babu and I were. As they pushed her through the door, she screamed, fell down, and all the demons immediately came out of her. God, the Holy Spirit, demonstrated the power over these demons to these Hindu "holy men," who were dishonoring the Name of Jesus. Then all the sick people began to push through the door, and many of them were healed of their sicknesses and diseases. Then the whole village said. "Ah! This Jesus, the God of the Christians, is much more powerful!" and they turned to the Lord, and many were delivered and saved. Even the Hindu priests repented and were converted; they were delivered of their demons and became followers of Jesus.

Whatever Is Born of God Overcomes the World

In 1 John 5:4, the apostle John writes, "Whatever is born of God overcomes the world." He did not say "whoever" but rather "whatever." Even if you do not feel human anymore, you are included here! It is not a matter of how you feel but whether or not you are born of God. You may feel as low as King David did, when he wrote in the prophetic Psalm 22:6 that "I am a worm and no man," as he saw Christ's crucifixion. The question is: Are you born of God? Say it aloud, "I'm born of God!" The NIV translation says, "For everyone born of God overcomes the world. This is the victory that has overcome the world, even our faith" (1 John 5:4 NIV). Everyone includes you!

You must believe in who you are, beloved. You must believe that when you invited the Holy Spirit to come to you He did come. However, He did not come just to give you a pleasant release in praise and worship and to speak in tongues, wonderful as these things are. But His purpose was to come and be a militant warrior in you and through you in His mission to war against the kingdom of darkness.

The Holy Spirit is implacably set against the prince of this world. In spite of the court order issued at Calvary in Jesus's favor, giving Him complete victory, the Devil continues to hold on aggressively to the remains of his tottering kingdom. The demons in your city have been fearfully waiting for some Christians to rise up and believe in who they are in the risen Lord Jesus Christ when filled with the Holy Spirit. When this happens, the demons know they are finished.

This is similar to the story of the people of Jericho when the city was completely shut up. Rahab said to the Jewish spies, "I don't know why it took you forty years to come here. We knew that once the children of God crossed the Red Sea that we were defeated. We have been nervously waiting for you to come ever since" (Josh. 2:10–11). The inhabitants still made a mighty fight of it, but they fought as those who already had a defeated heart, because they knew that Jehovah God was the victor.

> *For whatever is born of God overcomes the world. And this is the victory that has overcome the world—our faith. Who is he who overcomes the world, but he who believes that Jesus is the Son of God? This is He who came by water and blood—Jesus Christ; not only by water, but by water and blood. And it is the Spirit who bears witness, because the Spirit is truth.* (1 John 5:4–6)

We must see this biblical truth as a matter of faith. Years ago, in Bombay, we established a church in a predominantly Catholic area. It was the darkest, most evil, uninviting area I had ever seen. There was witchcraft and illegal drinking houses everywhere. In addition to that, every backyard was brewing its own liquor. Almost every man was constantly drunk. Old batteries were used to accelerate the fermentation rate, so there was a high lead content in the liquor. Men were dying of lead poisoning as well as drinking themselves silly. You could hear these drunken men beating up the women every night. I tell you, it was the nearest thing to hell on earth that I had ever experienced. It was a black, dark hell.

We lived there in that area for about two years in order to establish a church and see a breakthrough. With great difficulty, we grew to about forty people. Then the Devil launched an almighty counterattack against us. The Catholic authorities labeled us a dangerous sect and forbade anyone to have anything to do with us.

There were some who incited gangs to threaten us and abuse our people. They came and broke up our meetings. It became really ugly. In addition to that, the ruling demon physically assaulted me. One night while I was alone, this demon came and grabbed hold of me by the throat and tried to choke the life out of me. I found myself waking up in the night wrestling with this demon in bed. I thought at first a thief had broken into the house. When I came to myself, I realized the "thing" I was fighting with was not a thief or any human being but a demon.

Something in my spirit rose up against it. I can only assume it was the Spirit of God in me, and I heard myself roaring like a lion and shouting, "How dare you!" Suddenly this demon shrank down, lost its power, and was struggling to get away from me. A great boldness came upon me and I said, "I won't let you go!"

The demon slipped out of my grasp and went across the room. In Indian houses we did not have doors between the rooms, only curtains hanging in the doorways. As this demon went through the curtains, I leapt off my bed like a rocket. I used to be a rugby football player; it was my passion. I hit this thing with a flying tackle as it went through the curtains. I was amazed; I was not even scared, but simply indignant and angry that something like that would dare to attack me. I ended up with all the curtains falling down on top of me. When I had unraveled myself, this demon had disappeared.

On an earlier occasion, this same demon had tried to assault my wife, Eileen. It also attacked a fellow worker in a nearby house the same night. Through these experiences, God put steel into us. We were not going to run away. We were going to stay and fight and see the victory of our God.

It was only a few days later that we saw a mighty breakthrough, after we went to war in the spirit. We entered a new level of prayer, intercession, and spiritual warfare. That night something cracked in the heavenlies and the demon fled. I felt it happen. Immediately following that, we began to see an incredible harvest of people coming into the Kingdom. I am not exaggerating at all when I say that we saw a hundred thousand people saved and many healed of every kind of disease in a period of four years. Our only problem was finding enough time to eat in between leading entire families to Christ. They were knocking on our door and asking how they could be saved.

Eileen could not even go shopping without being bombarded by people saying, "Would you please come and pray for this sick person?" or others lamenting, "Oh, I desperately need to be saved!" One day, Eileen left the house just to stop at the store and returned hours later. She said, "I couldn't get away. I saw so many demons cast out, so many people saved, and so many people healed. And by the way, here are the things from the store!"

I said to her, "If this keeps going on like this, then we are going to die of exhaustion, but what a lovely way to die!" Amen!

When Jesus died, He overcame the world. Today through you, by faith, He still overcomes. If you will believe, you will overcome! Whatever is born of God overcomes the world, and this is the victory that overcomes the world—even our faith. Will you believe?

Precious Lord Jesus, Your death upon the cross encompassed every manner of life situation. You have left us without excuse. Your death has paid the price for our forgiveness for sin, delivered us from the power of the pull of the world, its evil system and control. Father, we hardly realize what You have done for us. Deepen our understanding of the Cross. Increase our faith and by Your grace enable us to live a crucified life.

CHAPTER 8

THE POWER OF THE CROSS TO RATIFY THE COVENANT—PART 1

To understand the functional power that makes all the benefits of the Cross become a great reality in our life, we will explore how the Cross ratifies the covenant relationship between mankind and his Creator God.

There are two words used in biblical writings for "covenant." The Hebrew word *beriyth* means "to cut or to slay," and this definition gives us insight into what covenant is about. Biblical covenant always involves the shedding of blood. The second word is from the Greek *diatheke*, which literally means "an unequal covenant." This is the word that is always used in the Greek New Testament to describe the covenant God has made with us.

An Equal Covenant

When two parties make an equal covenant, they discuss and agree, that is, negotiate the terms of that covenant, and each promises to take some action in consideration for what the other party is delivering. For example, they might agree that "if you do this or that then I will contribute this or that." They agree together on what the terms and conditions of the covenant will be. This is an equal covenant. Business contracts and peace treaties are equal covenants.

An Unequal Covenant

However, an unequal covenant occurs when terms are not negotiated and only one party must take action. For example, when someone, usually a king or a conqueror, states the terms and conditions of peace leading to a ceasefire, saying, "This is my deal. Take it or leave it!" the terms are not negotiated. Instead, the terms are stated by the conqueror or the benefactor. He would be the one offering the covenant. The other party to the covenant would simply be a beneficiary. The benefactor supplies all the terms and conditions and supplies all the power and resources to make the covenant work. The beneficiary simply says, "Yes, I receive the covenant on the terms you have decided," but they have no active part in the working out of that covenant. This is called an unequal covenant.

Now, in the New Testament, implicit in the Greek word for covenant, *diatheke*, is this idea of an unequal covenant. God has made such a covenant with mankind. He has established the terms and the conditions, the blessings and the curses. There is no negotiating. We can take it or leave it, but we can't change it. He will supply all the power and the resources to make the covenant work if we chose to accept the terms and conditions, but we cannot change them.

The Covenant Ceremony

Now I want you to see how in Old Testament times covenant ceremonies were conducted when two parties making a covenant slaughtered one or more animals. They would kill the animals by cutting them in half and dragging the two halves of the carcasses apart so that all the blood and guts flowed out on the ground. They would do the same with more animals, leaving a bloodstained path with the halves of the sacrificial animals on both sides of the path of blood. Then they would join arm in arm and walk down the covenant path, speaking a negative statement and a positive statement.

The negative statement would be something like this: "May God do to us, and much more than what has been done to these animals, if either of us breaks the terms or conditions of this covenant." In other words, if I break the terms of the covenant, then I am bringing judgment upon myself, worse judgment than what has been done to these animals. Understandably, people did not enter into a covenant lightly.

Then there would be a positive statement. They would join arms and walk down the covenant path saying something like this, "I will keep the terms of this covenant to the degree of the pouring out of my life blood, the way these animals have been sacrificed and have poured out their blood." In other words, the pouring out of their blood is representative of what I will do and how far I will go to make sure this covenant is kept. That means I am prepared to lay my life down, and have my life blood poured out, rather than break the terms or in any way fail to fulfill this covenant. That is the heart of the covenant.

Tragically, in our Western culture, we have lost the original concept of a covenant. Covenants are no longer made with the seriousness and consequences that were once inherent in the covenant agreement. While a covenant was a wonderful promise or guarantee, it was at the same time something to be fearful of taking lightly or breaking. As we meditate upon the covenant, may we gain deeper understanding of what God entered into at Calvary and, therefore, what He is looking for in our response as we covenant with Him.

There is another way a covenant was made, particularly a covenant between two men and their families. They would each first make a cut in their wrists. Second, they would press the two wrists together so that their two bloods were mixed. Finally, they would let a few drops of this mixed blood from the two wrists pressed together drip into a cup of wine. The blood and wine was stirred together, and then they would each drink from this "cup of the covenant."

Now you can see from where some of the imagery of the Lord's Supper comes. The drinking of the mixed wine sealed the covenant. Each of the participants from that day would have a scar on their wrist, reminding them of the covenant oath they had made with each other. This is probably the type of covenant that David and Jonathan made with one another.

One day, years later, after Jonathan had died and David had now become king, perhaps David looked down and saw the covenant scar on his wrist. This reminded him of his covenant with Jonathan, which had included any of his descendants. Immediately, David searched for Jonathan's remaining family members to whom he could show favor and kindness; he found Mephibosheth, Jonathan's son. (Read the story in 2 Samuel 9:1–13.)

The Covenant Seal

It is important that you understand the nature and seriousness of a covenant. The covenant represents a "seal" on a relationship. In our Western society, we have lost understanding and awe concerning a covenant, but in certain tribes in Africa and in other parts of the world, it is alive and well. Once a covenant has been made, it is impossible for those in a covenant to maintain any sense of self-respect if they do not honor the covenant.

I want us to look at how God develops covenant in scripture. In Genesis 15, we see God making a covenant with Abram. The covenant that God made with Abram is, of course, developed and ratified in our Lord Jesus Christ. It all began in Genesis 14, where we learn that Abram went to war with a covenant company of people. Genesis 14:14 says that "when Abram heard that his brother was taken captive, he armed his three hundred and eighteen trained servants, who were born in his own house, and went in pursuit as far as Dan." The entire story of Abram and the covenant community from his own household is a picture of the power of the covenant. Working together, they defeated the four kings. The church is a covenant community with God through our Lord Jesus Christ. Working together in the same manner, we too can defeat our enemies.

In this battle with the *four* kings, we see a covenant principle here of how God intends to defeat demonic principalities and powers. This is an important prophetic allegory speaking to our own experience of spiritual warfare because we must detect demonic principalities and powers that exercise rule and dominion over the earth. This theme is repeated in scripture several times. In the book of Joel, four locust armies devour the land. In the book of Zechariah, four strong horns or ruling powers go forth seeking to destroy God's people and scatter them. Everything is ruined and destroyed by them, and the tribes of Israel became weak and divided. In scripture, the number four is often used to prophetically refer to that which concerns the whole earth. This is a picture of the power and strength of demonic activity.

The Godly Heritage of America Is Under Attack

If you have anything in you that is spiritually alert, then you will recognize the demonic activity that is happening in the United States of America today. Our original, godly heritage is being ripped apart by a great demonic horde at this time. It is an invasion of immense proportions and it has been preceded for almost a century by *four* attacks following one after the other for many decades. They are as follows:

The attack upon the mind
The attack upon scripture
The attack upon morality and the family
The attack of materialism

Attack #1: The Attack Upon the Mind

The attack upon the mind began with the understanding of what I have already described earlier in this book; a philosophy of thinking, which is called "thesis–antithesis thinking." This is the philosophy of the Judeo-Christian world historically.

This philosophy is based on the belief that there are eternal rights and eternal wrongs established by God Himself. All that is not right in His sight is totally wrong and there is no good in it at all. In other words, there are black-and-white principles. There is absolute truth and all that is not of that truth is error. There are absolutes that are right and wrong. If they are wrong for one person, they are wrong for every person. That is called thesis–antithesis thinking. It accepts the fact that there is absolute truth and therefore that which is not of that truth must of necessity be an error.

That is the way we used to think. It was part of God's gift to our particular culture, but at the turn of the century, it was rejected by the "new thinkers." This "new" way of thinking started in France, moved across Germany, and then came across to America.

Every secular institution of education now uses a different method of thinking, called "synthetic thinking." Synthetic thinking means that you accept and listen to anyone who has a rational sincere opinion about anything. According to this philosophy, truth is slowly evolving out of a mishmash of all these different opinions. Therefore, there are no absolute truths anymore. You cannot say that anything is absolutely right or wrong because that is not intellectually satisfying.

If you have had any kind of advanced secular education, then you will have hit this head-on in your education. I thank God that shortly after I got saved He delivered me from my intellectual synthetic thinking and renewed my mind to think like God. I became a thesis–antithesis thinking person. If God said it was true, then it was true. If He didn't say it was true, then it was not true. If Jesus is the only way, then there is no other way. In doing this I was not abandoning my intellect, but on the contrary, I was thinking straight for the first time in my life.

But the invasion of synthetic thinking in our society has become so strong that a person is regarded as a bigoted fool if they have any strong, godly defined beliefs about anything. One of the results of this has been the destruction of strong leadership. If you have no God-given strong opinions about anything, then you have nothing to live or die for. That is why we have such a crisis of leadership today.

Attack #2: The Attack upon Scripture
The next thing that was attacked was the trustworthiness of scripture. Once you have people thinking synthetically, it is not hard to get them to question the truth and validity of scripture. Once they have begun questioning the words of scripture, they have lost their absolutes, and the Devil can introduce all kinds of false teaching and fill their imagination with anything he wants. He can change Christianity until it becomes unrecognizable. He can bring all kinds of cults and "isms" until open Satan worship is as acceptable as anything else including the celebration of a satanic mass.

Attack #3: The Attack upon Morality and the Family
Who would have thought that we would live to see "alternative life styles" accepted as normal? The slow erosion of biblical standards for family life and marriage has opened the door to a demonic assault upon the foundation of our society. As the erosion of standards wrecked their destruction, children grew up without security, a moral compass, character, and spiritual training. We live with the result every day—divorce, broken families, abuse, school dropouts, along with gender confusion, and so I could go on.

For decades, there has been a demeaning of fatherhood. The authority figure of the family has been made to seem incapable and of no importance. Men, understandably in this hostile society, back away from taking responsibility and as a result force their wives into a position where they are forced to organize family life for the sake of the children. As husbands and fathers abdicate from their positions, they leave a huge vacuum that the enemy has been quick to fill with every kind of moral corruption.

Attack #4: The Attack of Materialism

First, let us get a clear definition of materialism. It's a preoccupation or emphasis upon material things, including our comforts. Materialism brings with it a disinterest or rejection of spiritual, intellectual, and cultural values. It is encapsulated in "the lust of the flesh" included here in the love of money that the Bible says is the root of all evil. I have nothing against prosperity; it is God's will for us to prosper so that our surplus can be given into the Kingdom. Greed and avarice are dangerous, leading us away from God's purpose for our lives. Any yielding to fleshly appetites, whether it is focused upon luxury or compulsive lifestyles, or overspending on one's self for expensive pastimes; leads to a materialistic prison.

The American society seems trapped in this place; it has become one of the most materialist, money-loving nations on the face of the earth. As I travel and sit in restaurants and planes, I can usually hear people talking about money. Look at so many popular magazines and television shows and see the obsession with things. It is a great pollution of our nation. A simple lifestyle is no longer acceptable. Greed has taken over.

These four attacks, like the four great kings in Genesis 14, have come to dominate the land of the United States of America. The church, like the Hebrew people and through the power of the Cross, must turn the tide of these attacks.

In Genesis 14:7–24, God's people went against these four kings with five kings of their own but were defeated. Similarly, in the USA, the Church has largely been ineffective and has watched as these attacks have wreaked havoc in the country. For example, the Name of Jesus is not allowed to be mentioned in many American public schools by people in authority, whereas in the Czech Republic, Slovakia, Hungary, and Poland, formerly Communist nations, there is a wide-open door to preach Jesus Christ in the universities and schools. But in America, students are not permitted to hear about Jesus. This ought to stir some righteous indignation! We have sat around and let these things happen.

For too long, the church has looked for "celebrity evangelists," "celebrity preachers," and "celebrity teachers" to fight our battles for us and save the day. We expect *king-ministries* to go and win the nation for us while we play with a little church activity, without any real heart commitment.

The five kings went out against the four kings, but the four kings defeated them. When the five kings failed to destroy the four kings, they fell into their own slime pits. This is a dreadful allegorical picture of God's people being defeated because of their ungodly compromise and then drowning in their own filth. We have seen many so-called *king-ministries*, driven by human energy and compromised in their financial integrity, toppling into their own slime pits in our nation over the last few decades. In the process, they often bring great dishonor to the Name of our Lord Jesus. That is the work of Satan, but I also believe it is the chastening hand of God. The Church has left the battle to a few charismatic celebrity ministries when the whole Church should be engaged in the fight.

Then, out of this mess in Genesis 14, Abram was raised up as a covenant-man, the father–servant–head of a covenant community, the true family of God. This community of 318 warriors came under Abram's governmental father headship; they went out against these same four kings, types of demonic powers, but this time they were victorious!

God's answer to these great demonic ruling princes is the raising up of committed covenant communities who know how to get into divine order under proper God-appointed apostolic father–servant headship. They will go to war as a committed community and will pull down these kings. What the five kings could not do, Abram's covenant community successfully accomplished.

At the point when Abram slaughtered these four kings, the great High Priest Melchizedek could no longer stay in heaven. He said, "I've got go down to Earth to appear to this man Abram to bless him because this is a man right after My own heart."

So Melchizedek appeared to Abram and blessed him. Then Abram voluntarily, in love and faith, gave Him a tithe of everything. In response, Melchizedek gave him bread and wine. These are all symbols of the New Covenant. This experience, in theological terms, is called a "theophany," which is a pre-incarnate manifestation of the Lord Jesus, the Son of God, and there are several more of these in scripture.

If you read about the Melchizedek Priesthood throughout scripture, you will discover that in every mention it is described as a warring priesthood. The Melchizedek Priesthood is committed to pulling down and destroying all demonic resistance to the Kingdom of God! This is the priesthood to which we are called.

Now we come to Genesis 15:1: "After these things the word of the LORD came to Abram in a vision, saying, 'Do not be afraid, Abram. I *am* your shield, your exceedingly great reward.'" God was saying, "Abram, what you have just done is My strategy for taking the world back from the Devil and filling it with the glory of My Kingdom."

It is these covenant communities that will bring God's victory to realization. We cannot wait for some human "king" to come and fight on our behalf. We must form covenant communities that will destroy every demonic stronghold. We cannot wait for a great evangelist to come; we must work in God's ordained way, through covenant communities. God is committed to wiping the Devil off the face of the earth and destroying all of his works. Now, let us arise and work with Him.

God Initiates Covenant

A covenant is an agreement between two or more people, where they agree to keep certain promises. It is ratified by the spilling of blood and a sacrifice. There are two kinds of covenant: an equal and an unequal covenant. David's covenant with Jonathan was an equal covenant that included the promise to do good to their descendants so that David, when he became king, took Mephibosheth into his house.

When the Lord made a covenant with Abram, it was absolutely different; God made the terms of the covenant and all Abram needed to do was accept them. That is an unequal covenant.

The covenant with Abram is described in Genesis 15; here God says:

> *After these things, the word of the LORD came to Abram in a vision, saying, "Do not be afraid, Abram. I am your shield, your exceedingly great reward." But Abram said, "O Sovereign LORD, what will You give me seeing I go childless, and the heir of my house is Eliezer of Damascus?" Then Abram said, "Look, You have given me no offspring; indeed one born in my house will be my heir!" And behold, the word of the LORD came to him, saying, "This one shall not be your heir, but one who will come from your own body will be your heir." Then He brought him outside and said, "Look now toward heaven, and count the stars if you are able to number them." And He said to him, "So shall your descendants be." And he believed the LORD, and He accounted it to him for righteousness. Then He said to him, "I am the LORD, who brought you out of Ur of the Chaldeans to give you this land to inherit it." And he said, "LORD GOD, how shall I know that I will inherit it?" So He said to him, "Bring Me a three-year-old heifer, a three-year-old female goat, a three-year-old ram, a turtledove and a young pigeon." Then he brought all these to Him and cut them in two, down the middle and placed each piece opposite the other; but he did not cut the birds in two. (Gen. 15:1–10)*

Let me give you some of the principles here. As Abram prepared the sacrifice, the first thing that happened was that vultures came down and started attacking the carcasses of the slain animals. Abram drove them away. The vultures are a picture of the Devil endeavoring to rob us of the benefits of God's covenant with us. We must recognize that despite the Devil's activity he cannot stop God from keeping His covenant promise.

Someone may say, "Oh, there's a witch's coven started in my city!" or "We have one of the major New Age centers in our city!" Well, shut them down then through your prayers of faith! Do not worry about them because I tell you these spiritual vultures cannot keep God from fulfilling His covenant promise. So what does God do? He puts Abram to sleep (see Gen. 15:12)! Abram had to learn that God was going to keep His covenant because God is almighty and faithful. All that God needs is a suitable responder, one who receives, submits, and obeys—an expression of the fact that Abram had nothing to contribute to the making of the covenant.

This was an unequal covenant; while Abram was asleep, the burning oven of God's presence walked up and down the covenant path between the animal pieces (Gen. 15:17). It was God Himself walking the covenant path alone, saying, "By My power, by My life, and My glory, I'm going to make these things happen! And Abram, you just rest in faith. The Devil cannot stop Me from doing it!"

God Keeps Covenant

"How shall I know?" Abram asked.

God said, "You just rest, Abram. I will show you what covenant is all about! All the demons in hell cannot stop me. I have sworn by My Name. I have made covenant. I have committed Myself. These things are going to happen. Abram, your part is to receive by faith. It will be My power, My glory. It will be My faithfulness!"

In Genesis 17:1–5, the covenant continues to develop. God now invites Abram to respond:

> *When Abram was ninety-nine years old, the Lord appeared to him and said, "I am God Almighty; walk before me faithfully and be blameless. Then I will make my covenant between me and you and will greatly increase your numbers." Abram fell facedown, and God said to him, "As for me, this is my covenant with you: You will be the father of many nations. No longer will you be called Abram; your name will be Abraham, for I have made you a father of many nations."*

Now, if you are Abraham's seed, then this is your inheritance as one of his descendants. Just note in passing that the new name "Abraham" means "Father of a multitude" and implies a great and mighty harvest is going to be reaped by this seed!

God continues in Genesis 17:6–8:

> *I will make you exceedingly fruitful; and I will make nations of you, and kings shall come from you. And I will establish My covenant between Me and you and your descendants after you in their*

> *generations, for an everlasting covenant, to be God to you and your descendants after you. Also I give to you and your descendants after you the land in which you are a stranger, all the land of Canaan, as an everlasting possession; and I will be their God.*

The covenant that God made with Abraham was an everlasting covenant. The supernatural seed that produced Isaac has been "exceedingly fruitful," reaching to the nations and down time to our generation. The covenant that began in Abraham was ratified in Christ. The Abrahamic covenant was a shadow and a type; it foreshadowed Christ and His supernatural seed. The body of Christ is the full reality of this covenant. Through Christ we are of Abraham's seed, the descendants that were declared at the very beginning.

Circumcision: The Meaning of the Sign

God goes on to say to Abraham in Genesis 17:9–11:

> *As for you, you shall keep My covenant, you and your descendants after you throughout their generations. This is my covenant which you shall keep, between Me and you and your descendants after you: Every male child among you shall be circumcised; and you shall be circumcised in the flesh of your foreskins, and it shall be a sign of the covenant between Me and you.*

Have you ever thought about it or meditated on exactly why God chose this sign for the covenant? What does this mean? God is now asking Abraham for a response. Circumcision is to be Abraham's response to the covenant. All the power and all the faithfulness and initiatives come from God, but God is now taking Abraham one step further, saying, "I want you to circumcise yourself." It was a step that Abraham had to take himself. Once Abraham had obeyed, God said to him, "A year from now you are going to have a son" (Gen. 17:21).

Twenty-four years had gone by with God talking about a son. The moment Abraham came to this point of circumcision, God could speak to him of a definite time frame: "one year from now."

Let me say that if you respond to the spiritual equivalent of what circumcision represents then God will begin to talk to you about a definite time frame in which things will happen. Not one day, sometime in the future, but definite time frames. There are things that you have dreamed of, hoped for, prayed for, had faith for, and God wants to say to you, "This time next year…"

God Wants a Right Heart Relationship

The circumcision that God ultimately expects in response to His invitation for covenant is the circumcision of the heart. Let us reverently try and understand what this means. God has always been after a heart relationship with man. This is not just a New Testament idea; God spoke of it in the early pages of the Old Testament, but it was ratified by the Cross.

In Deuteronomy, we read the heart cry of God for our voluntary love:

> *Then the Lord your God will bring you to the land which your fathers possessed, and you shall possess it. He will prosper you and multiply you more than your fathers. And the Lord your God will circumcise your heart and the heart of your descendants, to love the Lord your God with all your heart and with all your soul that you may live (Deut. 30:5-6).*

> *I call heaven and earth as witnesses today against you, that I have set before you life and death, blessing and cursing; therefore choose life, that both you and your descendants may live; that your may love the Lord your God, that you may obey His voice, and that you may cling to Him, for His is your life and the length of your days; and that you may dwell in the land which the Lord swore to your fathers, to Abraham, Isaac, and Jacob, to give to Hem. (Deut. 30: 19-20)*

Can you hear the heart cry of God here? "Abraham, I want you to love Me voluntarily as your Father God. This is your part. I will supply all the power, all the functional grace, all the faithfulness; I will deal with the demonic, and I will make a way for you, Abraham. But what I want in return from you is your faithful love given to Me so that you fully serve Me as a son. That is what I want."

What did Jesus say was the first and greatest commandment? "You shall love the Lord your God with all your heart, with all your soul, and with all your mind. This is *the* first and great commandment" (Matt. 22:38).

This is what God has always been after. So, to illustrate this, God chose the organ a man has to use to enter into a covenant relationship with his wife. He said to him, "You must circumcise it." God could have done this any way He wanted, but we need to remember that through all of His glorious physical creation God was at the same time spelling out spiritual parables through these physical metaphors.

The full reality was the spiritual, but God carefully designed the physical to be a shadow or parable of that reality. God planned that one man should give himself to one woman for life in the covenant of marriage and that by physical union the two should become one flesh (Gen. 2:24).

The act by which the marriage covenant was to be sealed was that the man should enter into the woman and that he should continually renew the covenant by the on-going physical relationship of that one man with that one woman for the rest of their lives. In other words, that physical act was an act of covenant.

God designed a woman in this way so that as her husband penetrated her for the first time on their wedding night there was a breaking of the hymen and shedding of blood, which was the seal of the covenant.

I hope you won't mind me speaking in this detailed way, but the Bible is very frank in several places on these issues. Remember, the Bible also says, "To the pure all things are pure" (Titus 1:15). If we receive these things with a pure, sanctified mind, they become very precious to us. So God said to Abraham, "I want you to cut off the foreskin of that organ, and this will be a constant physical reminder to you of your giving of yourself in fidelity to Me."

Now God is Spirit and you can only love Him in spirit. God says, "All through your life, as you make love to your wife, because of this act of circumcision it will constantly remind you to be faithful to your wife. It will also remind you that spiritually I want you to have a circumcised heart relationship with Me. What you are spelling out in your relationship with your wife is a picture of the spiritual reality that I want you to be constantly living with Me." When you begin to see that, then you begin to see the incredible holiness of God's design in the covenant.

The New Testament Reality of Circumcision

We now go from the Old Testament outward sign of the covenant to the New Testament spiritual reality that it represents. Romans 2:28–29 says:

> *For he is not a Jew who is one outwardly, nor is circumcision that which is outward in the flesh; but he is a Jew who is one inwardly; and circumcision is that of the heart, in the Spirit, not in the letter; whose praise is not from men but from God.*

God has always cried out for men and women with circumcised hearts, who will give themselves to Him in the same fidelity that He requires of a man when he gives himself to a woman in the relationship of marriage. Remember, the reality is Christ and His Church or God and the believer; both are metaphors in scripture. The shadow is the husband and wife living out the marriage covenant together. The reality is the mystery between God and mankind in the Spirit. The physical act of circumcision is the shadow of that spiritual reality. I believe we need a desperate revelation of this. Why this particular organ? Because it sanctifies that act and constantly reminds us of the need to have a circumcised heart.

Colossians 2:9–12 goes further to explain this spiritual reality and even further to introduce the sacrament of baptism as part of the picture of our covenant with Christ:

> *For in Him dwells all the fullness of the Godhead bodily; and you are complete in Him, who is the head of all principality and power. In Him you were also circumcised with the circumcision made without hands, by putting off the body of the sins of the flesh, by the circumcision of Christ, buried with Him in baptism, in which you also were raised with Him through faith in the working of God, who raised Him from the dead.*

In this passage, the ordinance of baptism as a believer is clearly taught as an act of burial and an act of spiritual circumcision through which we are cut from our old nature and raised in the power of His resurrection life so as to be faithfully married to our Husband, the Lord Jesus Christ.

Taking communion at the time of your baptism is a wonderful thing to do, and it is like the first entering in of a man into a woman on their wedding day. From then on, every time we take communion, it should be like the constant renewing and reenacting of the covenant relationship that now exists between a believer and a Holy God. But if we take communion and regularly at the same time live unfaithfully in our holy covenant with God, then we will bring judgment upon ourselves.

Paul strongly warned the church in Corinth that many were sick and some had even died because they were taking communion in a way that was unholy and profaning its covenantal nature (1 Cor. 11:27–30). God requires us to corporately be the Bride of Christ, whether we are male or female.

As a young man, I was a rugby-playing, mountain-climbing, rough sort of person. I had very healthy normal male desires, but a few years after I had become a Christian, God really dealt with me over this issue of having a pure mind, and I received a wonderful deliverance from my unclean thinking. God has kept me pure in my mind ever since. I don't even think those unfaithful thoughts anymore, which were no less than spiritual adultery.

As I have explained in my earlier books, I didn't start out that way in my Christian life. During my rebellious, unconverted years, I read books and watched films that polluted my mind. When I went to India as a missionary, I was still struggling with an unclean mind. I cried out to God and when I got baptized in the Holy Spirit, I thought that would eliminate my unclean thoughts, but it didn't.

By then, I had been thoroughly taught by my evangelical tutors that I would always be struggling with unclean thoughts all the rest of my life because of my inherent, sinful nature. They had said, "You need to understand that you still have two natures, like two dogs inside of you—your old sinful nature and the new nature, and they are at war with each other. If you pray hard, the new nature will get stronger and most of the time it will win, but if you neglect your prayer life, the old nature will reassert itself and triumph over your new nature."

They taught me that in this life I would always have these two warring natures. It was God's means of keeping me humble. I was just to thank God for the blood because I could always go to Him and ask Him to forgive me for my sins committed during another week of failure. But I began to see that this was Judaism or law-bound religious Christianity and it was not what the Bible really taught.

I saw in scripture, after my baptism in the Holy Spirit, that God has given me the mind of Christ because 1 Corinthians 2:16 tells me, "For who has known the mind of the LORD that he may instruct Him? But we have the mind of Christ." The apostle Paul also wrote, "and that you put on the new man which was created according to God, in true righteousness and holiness" (Eph. 4:24) and "be transformed by the renewing of your mind" (Rom. 12:2). From these and many other scriptures, I began to realize that part of my inheritance was to have a new mind right now in this life. I had messed up my old mind pretty badly and needed a new one desperately.

One Wednesday morning, I came together with the Canadian brother I was working with in Bombay at the time and I said, "John, I'm having these battles with unclean thoughts. I can't even look at a beautiful woman without feeling embarrassed. I have never done anything wrong outwardly and I never intend to, but I've got to get the victory over these thoughts in my mind. I've been reading in the scriptures about having a new mind, and I see now that I can receive the mind of Christ as part of my inheritance as God's son. This morning I'm going to claim that new mind right now by faith in Jesus's Name."

I then prayed and prayed, and a demon of lust came out of me that morning although there were no violent manifestations as some experience. In saying this, I am not in any way discrediting what others have experienced. I took hold of God and His Word by violent and aggressive faith, and something broke off my mind that morning in the Baptist Church in Bombay, India, in 1965. I was free and able to receive a new mind. It is important to the Lord that His Bride is holy and pure.

I have been very careful ever since that day to guard this new mind and protect it all these years. I now have a pure mind because it's my spiritual birthright. God, in teaching us this mystery, uses all kinds of different parables out of the husband and wife relationship. At times, He speaks to us in our corporeity as the Church, His Bride, and He as the Husband. This is powerfully supported in scripture.

Be the Initiator. Come Boldly!
But God also showed me something else that almost astounded me. He instructed Abraham to circumcise himself because in the male and female relationship it is the man who is the initiator. It is the woman who is the responder. When a woman is in love with a man and they agree to marry, they must still maintain a pure and wonderful virgin relationship between them until the day of their marriage. The husband comes to her on their wedding night and she is open to receive him, and they meet each other in the deep intimacy of that initial union and they continue to love each other physically for the rest of their married life.

God has said to me, through these metaphors and parables, "I want you, and every other believer, man or woman, to come to Me like that in spirit. If you come to Me, with a circumcised heart, with faithfulness and fidelity, then I will be open to receive you." We are walking on delicate ground here, so please do not misunderstand me. I know the holiness of the things I am talking about.

God said to me, "If you will come to Me like that, with a circumcised heart, you can come right into the Holy of Holies of My being. You can know real intimacy with Me and I will show you My love, and My Father's love and the love of the Holy Spirit in a way you never thought possible in this life.

This is holy ground. You cannot come there without a circumcised heart. You cannot come there contaminated with the filth of the flesh. Our only approach can be with clean hands and a pure heart." (See Ps 24:4.)

This is what God wants to do in us. It is the relationship He longs for and is demonstrated in what He was doing with Abraham. That is why there is this great cry for pure, holy love in His heart. We must love Him in the way that He can receive it. He will not come down to the level of our fallen nature. We must be transformed and be raised to meet Him in His holy nature where He is.

I remember hearing a recorded message years ago, by Bob Mumford. He was having a time of prayer and fasting when God spoke to him, and

God said, "Mumford, you and I are incompatible, and I don't change!" I have never forgotten that remark. God is holy. If you want to live with God, you must become holy like God. He does not change. The writer to the Hebrews encourages us; Jesus has made what is impossible possible. Our High Priest has gone before us; we can be holy like God.

> *Therefore, brethren, we have boldness to enter into the holiest by the blood of Jesus, by a new and living way, which He hath consecrated for us, through the veil, that is to say, His flesh; And having a High Priest over the house of God, let us draw near with a true heart in full assurance of faith having our hearts sprinkled from an evil conscience and our bodies washed with pure water. Let us hold fast the confession of our hope without wavering, for He who has promised is faithful.* (Heb. 10:19–23)

When Jesus hung upon the Cross, He took all our sins in His body (1 Pet. 2:24). He somehow actually became sin for us (2 Cor. 5:21). This is a great mystery that no man fully understands. Jesus willingly became foul and filthy with all the sin of Adam's race as He hung upon the Cross, bearing all that sin and paying the full penalty for it all. When it was all done, He cried out, "It is finished!" (John 19:30).

The Greek word *teleos* used here was also used by a gladiator when he was fighting with an enemy warrior and made the killing thrust in a battle. It was not the cry of pain, it was not the cry of defeat, but it was the cry of victory, "It's finished!" It's all over. I've won! When a gladiator made that killing thrust and his adversary was slain and died in defeat, he would use the same Greek word *teleos* or the verb *teleo*: "It's finished!" So, like the victorious gladiator, Christ cried out, "It's finished!" The Bible says He then bowed his head and dismissed His spirit (John 19:30).

Jesus was the only Man ever to be in charge of His own execution. He chose the exact moment when it was right for Him to die. The centurion soldier, a cold-hearted executioner who had killed many men, had never seen anyone who was in charge of his own execution before. At the right time, Jesus bowed His head, dismissed His spirit, and died. The soldier looked up in awe and amazement and said, "Truly this man was the Son of God" (Mark 15:39).

As Jesus cried that triumphant cry, the Bible says the veil of the Temple was ripped from top to bottom. If you can receive this, it was like God's innermost being was torn open to let redeemed sinners, like you and me, enter into the very Holy of Holies, right into the heart of the holy God. If you come with a circumcised heart, God is wide open to receive you and take you into the depths of His eternal innermost being.

As the book of Hebrews says, you must have boldness! You must be the initiator here. You cannot hang around saying, "I'm not worthy. I'm not fit to go in." If you can come to faith about what the blood has done for you, if you have settled in your heart that by the grace of God, not by your own efforts, you are going to live this holy way, God will be open to you.

Oh, precious is the flow that makes us white as snow. No other fount I know, nothing but the blood of Jesus.

Father, we come to You amazed at the length and breadth and depth of the power of the blood of Jesus. Father, You chose Your spotless Lamb and He was slaughtered as the one atoning sacrifice for all sin for all time. Jesus, You set me free. I can hardly grasp what You have done. Thank You and praise You.

CHAPTER 9

THE POWER OF THE CROSS TO RATIFY THE COVENANT—PART 2

Holiness is Not Just a Good Idea

You can and must decide to be holy. In fact, you are commanded to be holy. Holiness is a decision you make, and then it becomes a life that you live. "Be holy, for I am holy" (1 Pet. 1:16). In other words, if you and God are going to live together in the riches of His Father-love, you had better be of the same nature and heart and become holy as He is holy.

Power-assisted steering is a good illustration of this. When you get into the driving seat of one of those big Mac trucks, you can turn that steering wheel with one finger, and those mighty wheels will turn at your touch providing the engine is running to supply the power. The wheels turn not because of your strength, but because of the power-assisted steering mechanism. But you still have to put your hands on the wheel and make your decision to turn them; otherwise nothing happens. To become holy requires your active will, but it also requires God's power to make it happen. You must cry out and say, "Oh God, I'm longing to be holy!" And God will say in response, "I will move all the power of Heaven to make you holy the moment you really decide you want to be holy!"

We Must Be Holy to Enjoy God

When we lived in Bombay, our water was not safe for drinking. One of our jobs each evening was to boil the next day's supply of drinking water. The water, when cooled, was stored in a plastic bucket. That particular plastic bucket was exclusively used for one specific purpose—drinking water. One day I was working on our car because it had broken down again. I needed a receptacle to drain the oil into while I removed the crankshaft. I came into the kitchen looking for a suitable container. I looked at that plastic bucket used exclusively for drinking water, and I was thinking to myself, *That is just what I need. I could use that bucket just this once and then I would clean it out again very carefully so that no one would ever know.*

But my wife, Eileen, saw me looking thoughtfully at the bucket and became suspicious, and she said, "What are you looking at that bucket for?"

So I said, "I need something to put the oil into temporarily, and I'll be very careful to clean it thoroughly afterward."

She said in a loud voice, "You are not having this bucket! It is kept exclusively for drinking water. I will not let you put dirty oil into this bucket, not even once!" She could have said, "This bucket is holy!" It was a perfect definition of what this word means. That is the essence of holiness. When I responded to God's clear call in scripture to be holy as He is holy, I made a decision that I would *only* be available for God's exclusive use; I would never be available for anything else. Not even once would I allow anything dirty to come into this sanctified vessel.

If you make the decision, to be holy for God, He will supply all the power of heaven to ratify your decision. You turn the steering wheel, and He will put all His power behind that heart intent. "Be holy for I am holy" (1 Pet. 1:16).

As Jesus cried out, "It is finished" and dismissed His Spirit, the veil of the Temple was torn from top to bottom to signify that the way into the Holiest of All was now open. How did the religious Jews respond? It was as if they stitched it all back up again. They would rather live behind a religious veil than pay the price of coming to Jesus. They refused to receive Him as their Messiah by whom they too could be made holy and permanently live in God's holy presence.

Circumcision, as introduced by God to Abraham, was a holy ordinance to be observed by all Jews. As I have stated, it is a parable speaking of the circumcision of the heart, which in turn declares that the flesh life is being crucified daily and that we are holy and consecrated to God.

We can understand why God watches jealously over marriages as they are a picture of the heavenly Bridegroom and His Bride. When the children of Israel forsook the Lord by going after other gods, the Lord called it adultery. Sadly, too many earthly marriages follow Israel's fallen ways. As the Bible says in 1 Corinthians 6:18, "Every sin that a man does is outside the body, but he who commits sexual immorality sins against his own body." All sexual sins and adultery are in total opposition to God's glorious plan to demonstrate His covenant love to mankind.

Beware of the Concision

As we conclude this subject, let's look at Philippians 3:1: "Finally, my brethren, rejoice in the Lord. To write the same things to you, to me indeed is not grievous, but for you it is safe. Beware of dogs, beware of evil workers, beware of the concision." The NIV says, "Beware of those mutilators of the flesh." I want to explain this word "concision" or "mutilators."

First of all, Philippians 3:1 says, "Beware of dogs." These spiritual "dogs" are the kind of people who are out to get you and tear you apart if you don't agree with them and their doctrine. They are likened in scripture to some of the Scribes and Pharisees in the days of Paul and Jesus. It goes on to say "beware of the concision." The Greek word used here is *katatome*, and it is only used once in all of scripture. This Greek word was commonly used to describe the way sex offenders were punished in Paul's day. Men found guilty of lust and rape would be punished by having their genitals mutilated, rendering them incapable of continuing to commit the crimes of which they had been convicted and making sexual intercourse impossible. It seems to be a shocking and strange word for Paul to choose. But he wants to make a powerful point.

Paul is likening this condition to those who had been brought up in the very tight religious system of the Jewish Law like he had. That religious system so mutilated the spirit of people that they became "evil workers," incapable of having a spiritual love life with God and showing or feeling any emotion as they worshipped Him. Even today in some religious church systems, leaders still frown strongly on any display of emotion. They would say, "Oh! Emotion! We mustn't have any of that kind of thing in our church services." But it is genuine. We are commanded by scripture to not quench the Holy Spirit. Paul himself was an example of such a law-bound person before his conversion, yet he became gloriously free and learned to love the Lord his God with all his heart, spirit, soul, and body.

As I have already said earlier, I was a British Baptist. I hardly even smiled in church, never mind leaping over the pews for joy. I never lay prostrate on the ground under the power of the Spirit, lost in God's presence crying out, "Jesus! Jesus!" I never knew the wonder of tears streaming down my face with the most indescribable joy flowing through me. I had been made part of the "concision" by several years of traditional Baptist and Brethren church life. I was taught what proper and respectable religion was. But Paul says, "Beware of the concision," because it will stop you being free to love God.

If you have had that kind of religious background and you are still not free, don't say, "Oh! That's just my personality." It is not! God can set you free to be an unashamed, uninhibited lover of God so that you can love Him with all your heart, with all your soul, with all your body, with all your mind, and with all your strength. If you have not found that liberty, then you may need prayer to get free.

I am an example of what God can do. I am naturally shy. I was a classic introvert, but I am delivered from the bondage of these things. I am now an unashamed lover of Jesus. I cannot tell you how much I love Jesus and how I love to express that with every part of my being.

The Insolubility of Covenant

> *For it is impossible for those who were once enlightened, and have tasted the heavenly gift, and have become partakers of the Holy Spirit, and have tasted the good word of God and the powers of the age to come, if they fall away, to renew them again to repentance, since they crucify again for themselves the Son of God, and put Him to an open shame.* (Heb. 6:4–6)

Would this be describing a believer or unbeliever? I can't read it any other way than seeing this person as a believer. This scripture is saying it is impossible for such people, believers, if they fall away, to renew themselves again to repentance since "they crucify again for themselves the Son of God and put Him to an open shame."

When Jesus stood before the crowd and Pontius Pilate said to them, "Behold, your king!" what did the people say? "We have no king but Caesar. We will not have this man to rule over us. Crucify him!" They made a decision. The decision was either to have Jesus as their absolute Lord and King or else not have Him at all.

The word that is used for "fall away" is the Greek word *parapipto*. It means "to tear up a contract or to break a covenant." *Parapipto* applies to us if we have made a covenantal agreement to be a servant of Jesus, to have Him as our Lord, to be a covenant lover of God, and then we change our mind and tear up the covenantal contract to go back into the world.

We are not talking about a temporary wavering through disappointment or offense but a definite irreversible decision. After many years of marriage with my precious wife, Eileen, I cannot say that things have always been perfectly smooth. We've had moments of breakdown in communication and relationship, but never have we ever thought of breaking our marriage covenant.

We can experience some temporary difficulties in our relationship with God. There are situations that are unexplainable, things that remain a mystery. There may be troubles, discouragement, and huge challenges to faith along the way, but if we keep our heart intent toward God because we are entirely His, then we will sort these things out, find repentance, and be fully reconciled to Him. But if we deliberately tear up the contract, then there is no help for us. Hebrews 6:4 describes a decision to tear up the contract as withdrawing from the covenant. If you really do that, then God says there is no further place for repentance.

Only God can know a person's heart. Only He knows the motivations and secret thoughts. However, when you've tasted all the blessings of the covenant, and then choose to reject it for some other "god" or some other purpose in life, then the scriptures make it plain that you do so at your own peril.

Of how much worse punishment, do you suppose, will he be thought worthy who has trampled the Son of God underfoot, counted the blood of the covenant by which he was sanctified a common thing, and insulted the Spirit of grace? (Heb. 10:29)

God has opened up the Holy of Holies; He has opened up His very being and is inviting you to come in, to be His intimate lover with nothing hidden between you. The blood of Jesus Christ has opened up the way for you through the veil of His flesh. God has given you privileges that even the angels do not have. Why would anyone turn their back on all this?

The bloodstained covenant path was not the blood of animals, but it was the blood of the Son of God Himself. It was the blood of Jesus Christ poured out for us. It is the blood of the all-merciful God, the One who loves us and is faithful, kind, and full of grace. He is the One who goes the "second mile" to draw us to Himself. This is our covenant God, and how dare we count that blood as an unholy thing despising it after having walked the bloodstained covenant path with Him.

It's a costly thing to turn your back on the covenant you made with God for an immoral physical relationship, for financial gain, or for a power play to get temporary prominence in some church or movement. God says, "How can you do such a thing?" When we lie and cheat and live immorally, we are in danger of trampling underfoot the very blood of the Son of God, despising the Spirit of Grace, and counting the blood of the covenant a common thing. Covenant is a serious matter with God!

I love God with all my heart. I have wonderful intimacy with Him. I cannot get over how much He loves me. I cannot describe to you the wonder and joy of my fellowship with Him. But at the same time, there is an awesome fear upon my life. I cry to God that by His grace I walk faithfully with Him all the days of my life.

Over my many years of ministry, I've seen some men tear up the contract, and I had never imagined they would do so. It has created godly fear in me, and I hope it is within you as well. Surely none of us wish to lose that Holy-of-Holies relationship with Him for some cheap temporary gain in this life. May you increasingly understand the seriousness of our covenant relationship, and may that knowledge keep you faithful to abide in it.

The Marriage Covenant

We won't understand the covenant of marriage or any other dimension of covenant until we have grasped in some measure the covenant God has made with us as we discussed in the last chapter. Understanding your relationship with God, as a covenant relationship, is *the key* to understanding all other relationships.

The covenant relationship of Christ and His church is the reality. As we look closely at marriage, we see what an amazing parable it is of the heavenly reality. Even the way in which a husband and wife relate in marriage is patterned upon the spiritual covenant.

If men want to know how to be good husbands, then they simply need to learn to live like Jesus lived with regard to His Church. The Bible says that husbands must love their wives as Christ loved the Church and gave Himself for her. Husbands must wash their wives with the water of the Word, and their first responsibility is to present her washed with the Word and filled up with all the fullness of God (Eph. 5:21–33).

Husband, your wife is your first responsibility! Present her without spot, wrinkle, or any other blemish. If you neglect her because of your ministry or any other reason, the day will come when you are confronted. God will say to you, "You have had a successful life, but how have you treated your wife?"

Wives must love their husbands and honor them the way the Church is called to honor Christ. This passage in Ephesians chapter 5 is like a compass; we simply need to look back at Christ and the Church as a guideline for us all.

Previously, we saw that the whole purpose and heart of God's covenant with man is expressed in the way that He poured His life blood out upon the ground at Calvary. There He established a covenant to bring us into intimacy with Himself. With a circumcised heart, we can enter into a deep relationship with God so that we truly know Him. There is no limit to how much God wants us to know Him. The pursuit of God is up to each of us.

Let me repeat again, however, that God requires us to take the initiative. This covenant relationship is something we must seek after. Jesus said, "If anyone is thirsty let him come to Me and drink" (John 7:37). Job asked the question, "Can you find God by searching for him?" (Job 11:7), and Jeremiah gives God's answer, "You shall find me when you search for me with all your heart!" (Jer. 29:13).

"Know" God First

The word in the New Testament for "knowing God" is the same word used for a man knowing his wife in intercourse. The same word is used in Matthew 1:25, when it says that Joseph did not know his wife Mary until after Jesus was born. It is exactly the same word that is used in John 17:3 where Jesus says, "This is eternal life, to *know* You, the only true God, and Jesus Christ, whom You have sent" (emphasis mine). Again and again, you will find the exhortation to this full, deep knowledge of God, and the Greek word usually used is *epinosis*, which means the full, all-around, deep intimate knowledge of God.

These are the last words of 2 Peter: "But grow in the grace and knowledge of our Lord and Savior Jesus Christ" (2 Peter 3:18a). He again says in the beginning of his second letter, "Grace and peace be multiplied to you in the knowledge of God and of Jesus our Lord" (2 Pet. 1:2). You see, you are not going to grow in grace and peace until you increase your intimacy with God. Let's make it our ambition this year to know the Father better and more deeply than we've ever known Him before.

This is the cry of the apostle Paul in Philippians 3:10: that "I may *know* Him." At the end of thirty years of incredible ministry, raising the dead, seeing the mightiest of miracles, and having the most amazing revelations such as being taken into the Third Heaven and receiving revelation that is not even lawful to talk about—after all that—he says, "that I may know Him and the power of His resurrection, and the fellowship of His sufferings, being conformed to His death."

God's heart is for you to know Him. He created you for love—to love Him with all your heart, all your mind, all your soul, and all your strength. The whole point of covenant is to bring you into that kind of intimacy through that blood poured out at Calvary.

Showing the Covenant of Marriage to the World

Let's now return to the covenant of marriage because marriage is the demonstration of the parable of that reality. Marriage is a high calling and it's an amazing privilege. If you get it right, it's the nearest thing to heaven on earth, but if you get it wrong, there is nothing more like hell on earth! 1 Corinthians 12:31 says, "I will show you the most excellent way." Love is "the most excellent way." Let's make it our ambition to so love each other that we have excellent marriages.

We want ourselves to be the example and our churches to be exceptional in this respect. The loudest message we can speak to the world at this time is to live successfully as husband and wife and to raise children in godly order. That will shout so loudly to the nation that all the humanistic nonsense that is being taught will pale away into insignificance. Marriages and families are in trouble; people are crying out for something that works and for real answers to their desperate needs.

Mutual Exclusion of Law and Grace

I want to point out a few things before digging deeper into the truths of the marriage covenant. Romans 7:1 says, "Do you not know, brothers—for I am speaking to men who know the Law—that the Law has authority over a man only as long as he lives?"

Suppose I was to come to your church with a surprise for the pastor. I telephone in advance and arrange for the purchase of the newest model Mercedes Benz. I plan to give it to him as a gift. This gift would cost a lot of money. Imagine that I take the pastor to the Mercedes dealer and introduce him to his new car, saying, "Brother, this is my love gift just for you."

He sees this wonderful brand-new Mercedes, and he says, "Wow! Alan. That must have cost you a lot of money?"

I respond, "Yes, it did."

He continues, "You know, Alan, I feel a bit embarrassed to take it from you as a free gift. Could I just pay a little bit toward it myself?" He removes from his wallet a hundred-dollar bill and says, "If you will take this as partial payment, I will feel much better."

How would I feel about that? Would I not feel that my graciousness was being insulted? Is not a hundred-dollar bill a stupid amount to try to pay for the newest and most modern Mercedes you can lay your hands on?

You must see your salvation either completely by grace, which is a free gift, or by Law, where you must pay the whole amount yourself. There is a total and mutual exclusion of Law and grace. You must make a choice to live in either one or the other.

The whole purpose of God's covenant is to bring us into such intimacy with Him that we literally become one spirit with Him. Just as in marriage we become one flesh with our spouse, so God wants us to live in one spirit with Him for "he who is joined to the Lord is one spirit with Him" (1 Cor. 6:17). We cannot be nearer or more intimate than that. That is what God has already obtained for us through the Cross. Access to such a life is already completely done for us by Christ's perfect sacrifice, and all that you and I need to do is to earnestly desire and receive it as a completely free gift. All the power and all the grace comes from God. All we need to do is keep our hearts set toward Him, and He will do everything else.

It is so easy to get into Law and be unable to receive the full benefit of God's grace. You and I do not deserve it, but that it is the nature of grace. Grace is the undeserved riches of God given to us as a free gift at Christ's expense.

GRACE = God's Riches At Christ's Expense

God's purpose in the covenant of grace is to give to us all that He is, and all that He has, as a free gift. We need to learn the nature of this covenant because it is the key to the proper functioning of other relationships. It is a serious matter with God. You cannot jump into covenant one week and then the next week jump out of it again. Grace, what a great gift! God has made it freely available to us so that we should be able to walk in covenant fellowship with Him. We can only keep our side of the covenant, which is to walk in submission and obedience to Him, by His grace.

Spiritual Adultery

> *For the woman who has a husband is bound by the law to her husband as long as he lives, but if the husband dies, she is released from the law of her husband. So then, if while her husband lives, she marries another man she will be called an adulteress; but if her husband dies she is free from that law (Rom. 7:2–3)*

The husband that is being described in Romans 7 is the Law. While you are married to the Law, the Law requires you to obey it. Those who live by the Law to try to earn their salvation live a religious life as opposed to a life married to Christ. The Bible calls this spiritual adultery. Each one of us has to decide whether we are going to live by grace or by the works of the Law. If you are trying to be married to Christ and, at the same time, trying to keep the Law, you are living in spiritual adultery. You must make up your mind as to whether you are going to be a religious or a grace-filled Christian. You must decide whether you are going to be the beneficiary of God's incredible goodness or whether you are going to try to earn your salvation in some other way.

When you have died to the Law, you are free from the rules that the Law previously imposed upon your life. Notice, as we read on in Romans 7:3, that if a woman marries another man while her husband is still alive, she is called an adulteress. But if her husband dies, she is released from that law and is not an adulteress even though she marries another man. However, verse 4 explains that we, believers, have died to the Law through Christ's death on the Cross and now we live in grace through Christ so that we might bear fruit for God. "Therefore, my brethren, you also have become dead to the law through the body of Christ, that you may be married to another—to Him who was raised from the dead, that we should bear fruit to God" (Rom. 7:4).

Most Christians' problems stem from the fact that they really don't know how good and powerful God really is. His thoughts toward us are good continually. His will is good, perfect, and acceptable. By stepping into our own will, we lose so much. None of us wants to do that.

In my early Christian life, I went through several stages before finally coming to this conclusion. Stage one was when I realized that I had to do God's will but thought I was going to lose out by doing so. Then, I felt compelled to do it because I didn't want to go to hell. Later, I came to the place where I realized that the most wonderful thing that could happen to me was to be in God's will all the time. Finally, I realized that the worst thing that could happen to me was to miss God's will for my life and end up doing my own thing instead.

There Is No Christian Widowhood

In the Spirit, there is no such thing as joyful widowhood, something many Christians get wrong. They say, "Oh! We are now free from the Law, brother. We can do whatever we like!" No, you can't! You are now married to another. In fact, the Bible says you are not free from the Law until you are actually married to Christ.

While my children were at home and spiritually not yet married to Christ, they were under the rules of the house. The television programs they watched and the music they listened to were carefully supervised. When they went out, it had to be with permission, and they had to be home well before 10:00 p.m. Once they had really met Jesus, fallen in love with Him, and were married to Christ, they came under the greater law of loving Him with all their hearts and living only to do His will. Once this happened, they no longer needed the house rules. Then they were free from these rules, married to Christ, and lived under the greater government of Christ's loving Headship.

When we are married to Christ, He demands more from us but also provides all the power and grace to be able to do what He is asking of us. We must banish the idea of a loose, sloppy, charismatic way of living, where we are free from the Law to do whatever we like. It is false Christian teaching that suggests we can "love Jesus" and live any way we want. No, we can't! We are only free from the Law to be married to another, who is Christ, and His standards are much higher.

See how this relationship is described as a marriage? By the Spirit, we love Him with all our heart and soul. We are intimate with Him. We press into Him with a circumcised heart, exploring and discovering all the majesty and glory of the One who loved us and gave Himself for us. We become so deeply in love with Him that the fruit of our union with Him is the glory and majesty of the very life of God flowing through us. It is the genuine fruit of the Spirit. Concentrating on loving Jesus, knowing Him, and being intimate with Him will produce all this wonderful fruit in abundance.

Father, may the Church hold dear the covenant that You have made with us through the Cross of Christ. May the covenant of marriage be proclaimed throughout the land. May the power of covenantal promises hold us secure in our walk with You in our marriages and life that in the end we shall be the spotless bride ready for the heavenly Bridegroom. To Your glory, Amen.

CHAPTER 10

The Power of the Cross to Heal and Deliver Us from All Pain and Sickness

Isaiah 53:4–5 is a powerful prophetic word anticipating the coming of Jesus. Isaiah saw how the Savior would take away every curse, including sickness, by His death on the Cross. It reads,

> *Surely He has borne our griefs (which can be translated pains) and carried our sorrows (that also means sicknesses); yet we esteemed Him stricken, smitten of God and afflicted. But He was wounded for our transgressions, He was bruised for our iniquities; the chastisement for our peace was upon Him, and by His stripes we are healed.*

A curse came upon all mankind because the first man, Adam, stepped out of submission to God's rule into independence. He had no intention of becoming a sinner but was deceived by Satan to think that he could become like God by developing his own inner resources.

Once Adam stepped out from under God's rule, Satan was immediately able to rule over this independent man and curse him with a threefold curse of sin, poverty, and sickness. This curse passed upon all men and then contaminated all of Creation. On the Cross, Jesus became a curse for us so we could be freed from every aspect of the curse that Satan had been able to impose upon all Adam's descendants (Gal. 3:13). In this chapter, we are concentrating on the curse of sickness.

What a wonder: Jesus has already paid the full price to deliver us from every pain and sickness. His glorious resurrection three days later is the indisputable proof that this is an accomplished fact. It is by faith we receive the results of Christ's death on the Cross.

The apostle Peter boldly declares that "by His stripes we have already been healed" (1 Pet. 2:24). Sickness is not normal or natural. It is a demonic invasion and perversion of God's perfect creative handiwork. Satan's purpose has always been to corrupt, steal, kill, and destroy.

In John 10:9–10, Jesus declares Himself to be the only true Door into the sheepfold. All who endeavor to come in some other way are thieves and robbers and who come only to steal, kill, and destroy. Jesus further declares Himself as the Good Shepherd who has come so that we might have life and have it more abundantly.

The Connection between Sickness and Demonic Activity

In the list of the gifts of the Holy Spirit, we see miracles, healings, and the ability to distinguish between spirits (1 Cor. 12:9–10). Additionally, Jesus sent His disciples out with the power to heal the sick, cleanse lepers, raise the dead, and cast out demons (Matt. 10:8). All of these gifts and this power are involved in bringing a person to the healing and wholeness that Jesus purchased for us on the Cross. The clear distinction between healing and miracles is not always obvious. When the Lord does a creative miracle, instantaneously He restores damaged or missing parts to the body. These spectacular physical signs are the sovereign miraculous work of our mighty God and are something separate from healing.

They are a sign that we rejoice in but cannot always expect. There was a mighty flow of these signs in Jesus's ministry, bringing conviction and salvation to multitudes. As soon as He was anointed, Jesus became the fulfillment of Isaiah's prophecy:

> Now when Jesus had come into Peter's house He saw his wife's mother lying sick with a fever. So He touched her hand and the fever left her. And she arose and served them. When evening had come they brought to Him many who were demon-possessed. And He cast out the spirits with a word, and healed all who were

sick, that it might be fulfilled which was spoken by Isaiah the prophet saying "He, Himself, took our infirmities and bore our sicknesses..." (Matt. 8:14–17; see also Isa. 53:3–5).

1 John 3:8b tells us, "For this purpose was the Son of God manifested that He might destroy all the works of the evil one." And in Acts 10:38, Peter summarized Jesus's ministry with these words: "Jesus went about doing good and healing all those who were oppressed by the Devil, for God was with Him." There is a clear connection between sickness and demonic activity, all of which Jesus dealt with on the Cross.

Jesus Sent His Disciples Out to Cast out Demons and to Heal the Sick

Jesus gave His disciples authority over every demon and over every sickness and disease (Luke 9:1–6; 10:17–20). They were sent out and told to heal the sick, to cast out demons, to raise the dead, and to declare that the Kingdom of God has come near. They returned excited with all the things that the Spirit of God had done through them. Jesus imparted to them His anointing for that ministry assignment, and they saw wonderful miracles happen.

Jesus did not just pray for people. He spoke directly to the demons causing the condition and commanded them to leave (e.g. Luke 13:10–13). There are so many examples of this in the scriptures. Jesus had such authority that He just needed to speak a word and the demon would immediately leave and the person would be healed instantly of whatever condition he or she had. Jesus never refused to heal anyone. He healed everyone who came to Him without exception (Mark 6:53–56).

Jesus had authority and functioned in this way not only because of His divine nature but also because of His obedient humanity as a man. He lived this way as an example that we can literally follow. He had this authority because He also was a man under authority (Luke 7:1–8).He was under the authority of the Father, doing only what He saw the Father doing in heaven (John 12:49; 14:10, 31). As a result, he just spoke a word and it was done. If we imitate His life, we can see the same results.

While Jesus was on earth, during his anointed three and a half years of ministry, He was living in the same humanity that Adam had lived in before the fall. Adam could have lived the same way if only he had remained perfectly submitted and obedient to God the Father like Jesus did every moment of His earthly life, and we can too. Casting out demons and healing the sick by the power of God was the first biblical manifestation of the Kingdom, and it still is. It has always been the cutting edge for forcefully advancing the Kingdom in the nations.

The Right Environment for Healing

To create the right environment for healings to take place, there are various factors that must be present. The life of Jesus demonstrated above all the importance of prayer. Again and again in the Gospels, we find Jesus in prayer. Even when surrounded by a multitude of needy people, He would withdraw alone to a mountain or a desert place and pray, often praying all night. As a direct result, the power of the Lord was present to heal (see Luke 5:16–25; 6:12).

His prayer life and the healing power that flowed from it resulted in His disciples asking Jesus to teach them how to pray (Luke 11:1). They obviously learned the importance of prayer from that teaching because, after Jesus ascended back to His father, in Acts chapter 1, the disciples were praying together before the Day of Pentecost. For the next ten days, 120 believers, including all the apostles, were in the upper room, praying. When the Day of Pentecost had fully come, the place where they were praying was shaken, and they were all filled with the Holy Spirit and spoke in many different tongues. Immediately following this, the whole City of Jerusalem was shaken and many signs, wonders, and healings were done at the hands of the Apostles (Acts 2:2, 4, 43; 4:31). The spirit of prayer was evident in the apostles' lives and the early church creating an environment for supernatural happenings.

Faith for Healing

The only reason Jesus ever gave in scripture for failure to see a healing or casting out an evil spirit was unbelief (Matt. 17:17–21). The *prayer of faith* will definitely heal the sick. *Prayers of sympathy* will not bring healing; it is only *the prayer of faith* that heals the sick (James 5:15).

Unbelief or any other contrary spirit must be removed from the environment where healing is needed. When Jesus was about to pray for the sick or raise the dead, He would first physically remove all unbelieving people and those with contrary spirits from the room before He ministered to the needy person. He did this when raising Jairus's daughter in Luke 8:40–42, 49–56, especially verse 51.

We also read how Jesus could do no great work in His own hometown of Nazareth because of their unbelief. It was so bad that Jesus marveled at it, and as a result, even He could do no great work there. He could only heal a few minor ailments (see Mark 6:1–6).

When Jesus went into the Temple in Jerusalem during the last week before He was crucified, He found the money changers in the Temple polluting the atmosphere. So He drove them out with a whip and overturned their money tables (Matt. 21:12–16). Then the lame and the sick came to Him and were healed, and the children danced for joy. Jesus called this perfect praise.

In Acts 9:32–42 and especially in verse 40, we read how Peter acted in faith. He was called to go to nearby Joppa to a precious woman who had just died. He found a large group of wailing women who had been mourning over the dead body of Tabitha for two days. Following the pattern of the Lord Jesus, he put them all out and then got on his knees, prayed, and called her back to life. She opened her eyes and sat up, and Peter presented her alive to the crowd, and their sorrow was turned to joy. The whole area of Joppa was shaken, and many believed because of this miracle.

Willing to Bring Healing

For healing power to flow through us, we must be a channel or vessel as Jesus was. Christians often pray for the Holy Spirit to fall on their city without the willingness to become the channel for His activity. We must be willing both to be used and to be conformed into Christ's image to be qualified as a channel for God's healing power. Jesus demonstrated the need for these two levels of willingness. He fully prepared the people as His vessels through which the Holy Spirit could move in the city. Then the Holy Spirit could come and convict the world of sin, righteousness, and judgment. Jesus explained this carefully to His disciples in John 16:6–16.

Matthew 9:35–10:38 reflects the agony of Jesus and the passion of His great desire to send laborers into their city because the fields were already ripe for harvest (the Greek word *ergatas* for laborer literally describes a skilled workman). To fulfill the conditions, the laborers sent out by Jesus had to be moved with strong compassion just like He was. They had to see people as He saw them. Though people had been miraculously healed, Jesus still saw that many of them were harassed, weary, and helpless—incapable of resisting the Devil's attacks and activity in their lives. These laborers, just like Jesus, had to long to release people and work patiently to totally liberate them from Satan's clutches. They had to be holy as He is holy and love righteousness and hate evil just as He did. Then these laborers would themselves be impregnable to the Devil, and with fearless authority, they could rise up and attack all the works of the evil one.

In Luke 10:1–19, we read the story of how after Jesus had sent out the twelve apostles, He then sent out another seventy (some manuscripts say seventy-two). They were not sent out as apostles but were sent as apostolic delegates, presumably under the oversight of the twelve apostles. They were not restricted to going only to the Jews, like the twelve had been, but they were sent out two by two to all the cities and villages where Jesus Himself would come. They went to the Jews, Samaritans, and Gentiles alike. Their commission was the same. They were to heal the sick, cast out the demons, and proclaim that the Kingdom of God had come.

> *After these things, the Lord appointed seventy others also and sent them two by two before His face into every city and place where he was about to go. Then, He said to them "The harvest is truly great but the laborers are few. Pray the Lord of the harvest to send out laborers into His harvest. Go your way; behold I send you out as lambs among wolves. Carry neither money bag, knapsack nor sandals; and greet no one along the way. But whatever house you enter, first say Peace to this house. And if a son of peace is there, your peace will rest on it; if not it will return to you. And*

remain in that house eating and drinking such things as they give, for the laborer is worthy of his wages. Do not go from house to house. Whatever city you enter and they receive you, eat such things as are set before you. And heal the sick there and say the Kingdom of God has come near to you". (Luke 10:1–9).

You can see from this great passage of scripture that these vessels or persons were appointed or chosen by Jesus Himself and sent to advance the Kingdom of God through healing and miracles, proclaiming the Gospel. Within a few short years, a multitude can be reached and a great harvest can be reaped just as Jesus promised.

Today, Jesus is sending His willing ones into every place where He is about to go. We need people who are willing *to pay the price* to become a clean channel for the Spirit of Jesus to flow through them. They have learned how to receive the power and faith from God and then pass it on as a free gift to bless others, giving all the honor and glory to Jesus for the amazing things He will do through them (see Eph. 1:15–23 and John 7: 37–39). Paying the price means being pure, righteous, clean, holy, and able to hear the voice of God in our hearts. As we have already seen, our ability to hear is directly proportional to our obedience.

Jesus said so many times that if we want to be great in the Kingdom of God, we must humble ourselves and become like little children. Peter also declared in Acts 3:12,16, "Why look so intently at us as if we healed this man?...And His Name, through faith in His Name, has made this man strong, whom you see and know. Yes, the faith which comes through Him has given him this perfect soundness in the presence of you all." And in Romans 11:36, Paul said that it's all of Him and from Him and through Him.

To come to this level of faith and to see such miracles happen, we must soak ourselves in the relevant scriptures until they become part of us, until we really believe and live in the truth they declare. Soak yourselves in Ephesians, especially Ephesians 1:1–2:8.

You have to know who you are in Him and what He has become in you and that you are now seated together with Him (literally in Him) in heavenly places far above all principalities and powers with all of them under your feet. What you have received is entirely a free gift of grace. (See also

Acts 9:32–35 and 2 Kings 4:1–7.) Then by an act of faith, you give what you have received.

We spiritually have to learn how to continually eat of Him as the true bread that came down from heaven and drink the new wine of His resurrection life in His blood. Jesus taught these things in His great upper-room discourse recorded in John chapters 11–14. We must also continually drink of Him as living water as He taught us in John 7:37–39, which reads:

On the last day, that great day of the feast, Jesus stood and cried out, saying, if anyone thirsts, let him come to Me and drink. He who believes in Me, as the scriptures have said, out of his heart will flow rivers of living water. But this He spoke concerning the Spirit, whom those believing in Him would receive, for the Holy Spirit was not yet given, because Jesus was not yet glorified.

Note all the verbs in this passage of scripture are in the present-continuous tense. This means it is a current and ongoing action. These rivers of living waters continually flow out of us to the needy people all around as we continually drink of Him. We have to learn to release what we have received; the Holy Spirit trains and teaches us. This requires perseverance and obedience. We all make mistakes, but the important thing is to be willing to receive correction and learn from our mistakes. Don't expect to get there all at once, but do expect to make progress all the time.

Paul describes his own journey in the following words in Philippians 3:7–17:

But what things were gain to me, these I have counted them loss for Christ. Yet indeed I also counted all things loss for the excellence of the knowledge of Christ Jesus my Lord for whom I have suffered the loss of all things and count them as rubbish that I might gain Christ and be found in Him, not having my own righteousness which is from the law but that which is through faith in Christ, the righteousness which is from God by faith; that I may know Him and power of His resurrection and the fellowship of His sufferings being made conformable to His death, if by any means I may attain to the resurrection from the dead.

> Not that I have already attained or am already perfected. But I press on, that I may lay hold of that for which Christ Jesus has also laid hold of me. Brethren I do not count myself to have apprehended; but one thing I do, forgetting those things which are behind and reaching forward to those things which are ahead, I press towards the goal for the prize of the upward call of God in Christ Jesus. Therefore, let us, as many as are mature, have this mind, and if in anything you think otherwise, God will reveal even this to you. Nevertheless, to the degree that we have already obtained, let us walk by the same rule, let us be of the same mind. Brethren, join in following my example and note those who so walk as you have us for a pattern.

Receiving and maintaining a healing

Faith is the key. Our faith must be grounded in the completed work, power, and total victory of the Cross. We must walk by faith and not by sight, and sometimes we have to refuse to believe what our natural eyes are telling us. Faith is the substance of things hoped for and the evidence of things not seen (Heb. 11:1).

Luke 8:43–48, the story of the woman with the issue of blood, is a great example. She already had her healing by faith before there was any change in her body. She was sure that if only she could just touch the hem of His garment she would be healed. When she did manage to touch His garment, Jesus immediately felt the power go out from Him. Many others were touching Him, but her touch was a touch of faith, and Jesus knew the difference. He said to her, "Daughter be of good cheer, your faith has made you well. Go in peace." You can have your own "obtaining faith" like this woman had, or you can just be the beneficiary of another person's faith, like the vast majority that Jesus healed.

It is a tragic fact that many people lose their healing after they leave the healing meeting because the Devil comes, attacks them with doubt, and steals their healing from them. Jesus still saw the multitudes that He had just healed as harassed and helpless until the laborers had come and established them as true believers in their own right. The Devil cannot steal from people grounded in faith. They know what they already have, even when it is not manifested.

Seek to grow in faith believing God's Word and trusting Him to do you good. His desire is to heal you; by His stripes you were healed. Be healed, and be a conduit of faith and healing in your world.

Father, we thank You and praise You mighty God that You sent Jesus to bear our sicknesses, pains, and infirmities. By faith we grasp this truth and receive Your grace to walk in the health that Jesus our Healer gives us through the power of the Cross.

CHAPTER 11

THE POWER OF THE CROSS TO OVERCOME POVERTY

For you know the grace of our Lord Jesus Christ, that though He was rich, yet for your sakes He became poor, that you through His poverty might become rich. (2 Cor. 8:9)

Released from the Curse of Poverty

This verse is clearly talking about material riches and financial matters; we must read it in this way. The curse of poverty is broken from our lives by our faithful, sincere obedience to the principles of tithing and giving as we have examined closely. And I repeat: this obedience is not of law but a response of true love.

The whole line of the seed runs from Abraham, Isaac, Jacob (Israel), Joseph, David, and Solomon—right through to Jesus and the Church, which is now the one final corporate seed (see Gal. 3:16–29). All of these men were rich materially as well as blessed spiritually; only Jesus was poor.

God has always blessed nations, both spiritually and materially, that fear and honor Him. He has raised these nations to economic prosperity and power in the earth so that they may have bountiful resources to give abundantly according to His will to the needs of the world's suffering.

Poverty is a curse. There is nothing virtuous or spiritual about being poor any more than there is anything virtuous or spiritual about living in sin or living in constant sickness. Living in poverty is an insult to God's fatherhood. It was never His plan.

Jesus took the curse of sin on our behalf at the Cross to free us from sin just like He took the curse of sicknesses on our behalf to free us from sickness and disease (see 1 Pet. 2:24, 2 Cor. 5:21, Isa. 53:4). He also took the curse of poverty to free us so that we might become rich through him (see Gal. 3:13, 2 Cor. 8:9). Everything that Christ obtained for us by the power of the Cross is appropriated through faith.

To be delivered from the curse of poverty, we must have a Kingdom mind-set, with our minds completely delivered from worldly thinking as already described earlier in this book. The proof would be that we live in the Spirit and not in the flesh, living each day in the power of His resurrection life and seated together with Jesus on His mighty throne, from where we can rule over our economic circumstances. In that glorious place, the evil one and the curse of poverty cannot touch us. Then, when our finances are truly *kingdomized,* money can become a powerful weapon for forcefully advancing the Kingdom.

The curse of poverty is dispelled by simple obedience to the principle of tithing, giving, and having a generous heart. For those who wish to experience victory over poverty, they must tithe in faith and joy like Abraham our Father (Gen. 14:18–23). In so doing, they fulfill the conditions of Malachi 3:8–12, so they can experience the blessings that are promised there.

> *Will a man rob God? Yet you have robbed Me! But you say, "In what way have we robbed You?" In tithes and offerings. You are cursed with a curse, for you have robbed Me, even this whole nation. Bring all the tithes into the storehouse, that there may be food in My house, and try Me now in this, says the Lord of hosts, If I will not open for you the windows of heaven and pour out for you such blessing that there will not be room enough to receive it. And I will rebuke the devourer for your sakes, so that he will not destroy the fruit of your ground, nor shall the vine fail to bear fruit for you in the field, says the Lord of hosts; And all nations will call you blessed, for you will be a delightful land, says the Lord of hosts. (Mal. 3:8–12)*

By following these principles set out in the Old Testament and confirmed in the New Testament, we put ourselves under the blessing of God. And by living in the New Testament "Law of Giving" as spelled out by Jesus in Luke 6:38, where it says, "Give, and it will be given to you: good measure, pressed down, shaken together, and running over will be put into your bosom. For with the same measure that you use, it will be measured back to you." Then we shall experience the full blessing of what God has promised us financially and, as we use our resources wisely, help advance the Kingdom of God.

There is yet more to discover. The full "Grace of Giving" goes beyond even the New Testament "Law of Giving." Here we will experience having sufficiency for ourselves and the abundance for every good work that Paul spoke about in 2 Corinthians 9:7,8,10,11 (ESV).

> *You should each give, then, as you have decided, not with regret or out of a sense of duty; for God loves the one who gives gladly. And God is able to give you more than you need, so that you will always have all you need for yourselves and more than enough for every good cause. And God, who supplies seed for the sower and bread to eat, will also supply you with all the seed you need and will make it grow and produce a rich harvest from your generosity. He will always make you rich enough to be generous at all times, so that many will thank God for your gifts which they receive from us.*

As we embrace the truth of these words, we find the key allowing us to become great givers into the financial needs of many ministries and missions. We become partners in the work, forcefully advancing the Kingdom in many countries.

Tithes and Offerings

We can learn how to make money a blessing in the Kingdom of God through our tithes and offerings. Real faith-filled New Testament tithing all started with Abraham long before the Law was given. He is the father of all those who believe, and we are his sons if we have his faith (Gal. 3:7). We are the one corporate Seed that inherits the promises (Gal. 3:16, 29).

Let us examine how tithing began and was practiced in the Old Testament. The tithes given by Abraham to Melchizedek were voluntary tithes and preceded Moses's tithing of the Law (Gen. 14:18–24) by about four hundred years. Abraham's tithing had the following important qualities:

1) It was voluntary.
2) It was out of gratitude and joy.
3) It was of faith.
4) As a result, Abraham expected to be made rich (Gen. 14:23).
5) It was New Covenant in type after the order of the Melchizedek Priesthood (Heb. 7:1–21) and not the Levitical Priesthood.

The Tithing of Jacob (Gen. 28:10–22)

Jacob did not have the faith of Abraham, his grandfather. He was fearful and hesitant to walk the same way. He knew of the lifestyle of his grandfather and possibly his father but was afraid to try it. Fear always kills faith. We have to make a choice as to what kind of person we are going to be: a person of faith or a person of fear.

Jacob made a conditional commitment to try tithing (Gen. 28:20–22). He basically said, "If God will be with me and bless me in every way then He will be my God…then I will give him a tithe of all that I have." In other words, "After God has visibly blessed me, and I know I have enough for myself, then I will give some of it back afterward, when I'm sure I already have my own needs met." There is no faith in this kind of giving; only gratitude.

Tithing under Moses

During the forty years that Moses journeyed with the children of Israel, the voluntary love, joy, and faith went out of tithing. It became a legal requirement. The Levitical priests were commanded to take tithes from the people (Heb. 7:5). We learn from the period when Jesus was walking in Galilee that an increasingly complicated network of rules was developed by the Levitical Priesthood to extract the maximum tithes from an unwilling people. The people, however, looked for every legal loophole to wriggle out of as much giving as possible. Many Scribes and doctors of the Law became "Tithe Consultants." For a fee, they would help people to reduce their legal tithe liability! All this demonstrated the inability of the Law to produce real giving any more than it could produce real righteousness or faith.

The Law May Not Make Us Righteous, but the Principles Remain

Paul explains to Gentile Christians that the Law itself was not evil but good and holy (Rom. 7:12). The Law was given to reveal the evilness of the human heart and the weakness of the flesh. The Law revealed the sinfulness of sin but provided no cure (Rom. 7:7–12).

Christ is the end of the Law for Righteousness to those who believe (Rom. 10:4). The Law is not a means of obtaining righteousness, but it is still a way to teach principles that are an unchangeable part of the heart of God.

Jesus Did Not Come to Destroy the Law But to Fulfill It

Jesus superseded the Law by lifting it to a higher level (Matt. 5:17–20). Every principle of Law expresses something of the true heart of God and teaches us something that is carried over into the New Covenant in the joy of faith and the power of Christ's risen life. Grace-filled, joyful giving goes way beyond the Law and cannot possibly come short of it (Matt. 5:20).

Biblical Teachings Concerning the Tithes and Offerings

There are many passages of scripture teaching about tithes and offerings. It takes some time to extract all that the Bible has to say on the subject. To study more about this issue, reference important passages from the Old and New Testaments as noted in the footnote.

Under the law in the Old Testament, tithing covered every aspect of life. The literal tenth, the top of the pile, was given to support the Levites, who gave themselves full time to serving God and the people, and they, in turn, gave a tenth to support the priests. These were the actual members of Aaron's family.

In Deuteronomy 14:22–26, we learn of a second tithe. This tithe was set aside by the people to spend on themselves so they could attend the special festivals and holy convocations. This tithe was commanded in their yearly budgeting for the purpose of enjoying special times of spiritual and physical refreshment.

Yet another tithe in Deuteronomy 14:28–29 was required once every three years. It was used to support the widows, orphans, needy strangers, and retired Levites. So in total we see that each Law-abiding member of the nation of Israel tithed 23.333 percent of their annual income for these purposes.

Additional Giving and Special Offerings

In addition to the tithes, in Matthew 17:24–27, we learn that each Hebrew gave various other taxes such as the Temple tax, a half-shekel equivalent to about three days' wages. This supplied enough money to physically maintain the Temple and its functions. When special funds were needed to build a building or perform extensive restoration on the Temple in Jerusalem, a special offering was taken: for example, the building of the Temple under King David (1 Chron. 29:1–20) or the restoring the Temple under Joash (2 Chron. 24:1–14). The tithes were never used for this purpose.

Additional, voluntary offerings were given over and above all of the legal requirements to express gratitude and thankfulness to God. To withhold these tithes and offerings was viewed as robbing God (Mal. 3:8–9).

Tithing Is a Heart Issue

The failure to bring tithes was always the first indication that the people's hearts were no longer right toward God. Consequently, it was always the first thing to be restored in times of restoration (e.g., restoration under Hezekiah and Nehemiah). Malachi, the last of the Old Testament restoration prophets, declared that God's people had become thieves by keeping back for themselves what belonged to God in terms of tithes and offerings.

This led to the Devil being legally able to devour their substance and inflict all kinds of misery upon them. God could not protect them because they had put themselves under the Devil's curse by their disobedience.

God challenged the people through the prophet Malachi as he spoke in Malachi 3:10–12 (quoted at the beginning of this chapter). The challenge demands our obedience, and then God can legally and joyfully run to our aid. After these words in Malachi, there was a prophetic silence for over four hundred years until John the Baptist came announcing the coming of the Messiah.

The "Law" of Giving in the New Testament

Everything in the New Testament supersedes and exceeds the standards of the Old Testament (see Matt. 5:20–22). Spiritual laws operate through a changed heart rather than the external rules and regulation of the Law. These spiritual laws are unchanging, reliable, and relentless just like the physical laws of this universe. They always work for anyone, anytime, anywhere, just like the law of gravity. Luke 6:38, quoted earlier in the chapter, tells us that in the same measure in which we give it will be given back to us by God through men.

And Paul states the same principle when he says in Galatians 6:9, "Do not be deceived, God is not mocked; for whatever a man sows, that he will also reap." And in 2 Corinthians 9:6, Paul writes, "But this I say, He who sows sparingly will also reap sparingly, and he who sows bountifully will also reap bountifully." It is a generous and obedient heart that receives blessings from the Lord.

Money is not evil, but the love of money is the root of all evil.

Many scriptures in the New Testament teach a right stewardship of finances. Wisdom and right stewardship of our finances will lead us to use them for the Kingdom and not for our own personal gain and also earn us an eternal reward (see Luke 16:10–12).

We are promised *sufficiency* in all things for ourselves but *abundance* for every good work. The standard for ourselves is enough of everything. All our *needs* but not our *greed* will be met. If we truly desire to have the resources to bless the good work others are doing, then God will give us abundant seeds to sow into their ministry.

The desire to embrace the "Grace of Giving" goes even further than the New Testament "Law of Giving." The heart must be changed by supernatural grace. This is a glorious activity of the Holy Spirit. Remember and live Jesus's words that it is more blessed to give than to receive (see Acts 20:33–35). I believe that until we become loving, generous givers like God our Heavenly Father God has to restrict his giving to us because it would corrupt us. How we need our hearts to be changed by supernatural grace.

God's eternal life is, by nature, a life of extravagant giving. If you want eternal life, and all the dimensions of this wonderful life, you will find yourself being changed into an extravagant giver. You must be willing to give your all for the Lord (see Mark 10:17–31) to receive all He has for you. The condition of our hearts is the all-important factor, and He has the power to change our hearts.

It is very possible to be blessed with the abundance of resources because of faithful giving according to the divine principles set out so clearly in scripture. The Law works relentlessly like gravity, but without change of heart, this abundance is dangerous, and the financial blessing it brings can actually become a curse and destroy us if we still have a natural selfish heart. If our heart has not been changed, the more we have, the more difficulty we will find in giving when we come to understand the Kingdom and its government. We discover that we are challenged to give way beyond the minimum legal amount demanded by the Law of Moses. Kingdom-giving is sacrificial and to the point where our faith is really stretched. That is why it is so hard for a rich man with a natural heart to enter the Kingdom of God. If we "have everything" like Peter, that is, live free from the desire and control of material things and also have a heart of extravagant giving, then God can bless us materially with a hundredfold in this life, and it will not harm us. In addition, we can actually live in this world with the blessing of God's eternal life flowing through us so that we are thoroughly blessed and a blessing to many around us.

In the story in Mark's Gospel, chapter 12:41–44, we read how Jesus was watching as people gave their gifts in the Temple. Jesus is deeply concerned, and He carefully watches our giving as it is a true indicator of where our heart is. He measures not the quantitative amount but the sacrifice, love, and faith involved in our giving. In Mark's Gospel, the rich man gave much more quantitatively, with a showy display, than the poor widow. Jesus observed that while the rich man gave a large sum, it didn't really cost him anything. It was a fraction of what he possessed. On the other hand, the poor widow gave only one small coin, but it was everything she had. She made the decision that she would rather give than eat.

Seeing her giving heart, I'm sure God changed her economic situation so as to fulfill her heart's desire. I believe her decision to make this gift was the beginning of a change in her economic circumstances. I've seen this happen a number of times to very poor people in India who had behaved just like this widow. As a direct result of their heart-giving, God removed the curse of poverty over their lives and even over their village. I could tell many wonderful stories of how individual giving hearts have blessed the whole region, where they lived with a new economic prosperity.

It was the will of the Father to give His only beloved son, Jesus, who chose to do the Father's will and give His very own life as a sacrifice to save sinners. He would rather give than live. This is the nature of Eternal Life and the power of the Cross.

Grace to Be a Supernatural Giver

The grace to be a supernatural giver goes far beyond the laws of giving even in the New Testament. Paul speaks of this in his second letter to the Corinthians and encourages the believers there to act as the Macedonian church had responded:

> *And now, brothers and sisters, we want you to know about the grace that God has given the Macedonian churches. In the midst of a very severe trial, their overflowing joy and their extreme poverty welled up in rich generosity. For I testify that they gave as much as they were able, and even beyond their ability. Entirely on their own, they urgently pleaded with us for the privilege of sharing in this service to the Lord's people. And they exceeded our expectations: They gave themselves first of all to the Lord, and then by the will of God also to us. So we urged Titus, just as he had earlier made a beginning, to bring also to completion this act*

of grace on your part. But since you excel in everything—in faith, in speech, in knowledge, in complete earnestness and in the love we have kindled in you—see that you also excel in this grace of giving. (2 Cor. 8:1–7)

A supernatural giver yearns to give and lives to give. They long for greater resources in order to give more, not to have more. Their heart is revealed when they only have very little and still feel compelled to continue giving to the point that it costs everything. People with this gift of giving cannot wait until once again there is sufficiency to give (see Rom. 12:8).

Supernatural grace for giving filled the heart of the poor widow and corporately upon the Macedonian church but not the Corinthian. Whole regions or even nations can be blessed by a spirit of grace to give, or conversely, they can be impoverished by a spirit of poverty, followed by meanness and covetousness because they never respond in *real* giving. By this grace, we can experience the same heart that Jesus had when He said, "It is more blessed to give than it is to receive" (Acts 20:35). He was declaring His own heart as He willingly went to the Cross and gave His all for us.

Grace to Receive Abundance of Supply

As we have already seen, the release of this grace is conditional and not automatic. To be able to receive this grace, the heart must be changed. Once the heart has been changed by grace, it longs to be a generous and cheerful giver, and then it is safe for God to release the resources that can satisfy the heart's desire (see 2 Cor. 9:6–8).

These grace-filled givers pour out financial abundance in daring, faith-filled giving, releasing these resources according to God's will. The abundance they receive is not to be consumed on themselves, but is for every good work, that is, to bless all men, especially God's people, and to give generously into the work of the Kingdom. Here we see the scripture fulfilled, "Give, and it will be given to you: good measure, pressed down, shaken together, and running over will be put into your bosom. For with the same measure that you use, it will be measured back to you" (Luke 6:38). Those who give like this, whether very wealthy or even those considered poor, will always have sufficiency for themselves. The Christian who receives the grace of God to give will never be in need except on the rare occasion when for a period of time faith is being tested. All faith has to be tested to prove it is genuine and to develop it and make it grow stronger.

Will You Sow or Eat Your Resources?

> *Whoever sows sparingly will also reap sparingly and whoever sows generously will also reap generously. Each of you should give what you have decided in your heart to give, not reluctantly or under compulsion, for God loves a cheerful giver. And God is able to bless you abundantly, so that in all things at all times, having all that you need, you will abound in every good work. As it is written: "They have freely scattered their gifts to the poor; their righteousness endures forever." Now he who supplies seed to the sower and bread for food will also supply and increase your store of seed and will enlarge the harvest of your righteousness. You will be enriched in every way so that you can be generous on every occasion, and through us your generosity will result in thanksgiving to God. This service that you perform is not only supplying the needs of the Lord's people but is also overflowing in many expressions of thanks to God. Because of the service by which you have proved yourselves, others will praise God for the obedience that accompanies your confession of the gospel of Christ, and for your generosity in sharing with them and with everyone else. And in their prayers for you their hearts will go out to you, because of the surpassing grace God has given you. Thanks be to God for his indescribable gift! (2 Cor. 9:6–15)*

In India, until recently, most farming was still carried on in much the same way as we read it was done in biblical times. They used wooden ploughs pulled by yokes of oxen. At harvest time, the same oxen were then used to tread out the grain on threshing floors identical to the ones described in the Bible.

When a small peasant farmer had reaped a harvest, he had to be careful to provide for the next year's seed. His first concern would be to set aside some of the grain for sowing. As a first priority, especially in a lean year, he kept back the best grain for seed or there would be no harvest the following year.

What an application there is for us here as we consider our attitude to bringing our tithes and offerings to God. These can be likened to seed; if we don't sow, we have no harvest. Even in lean years, we need to preserve seed for sowing.

We can choose to practice *maintenance sowing* or we can multiply our resources through *abundant sowing* (see 2 Cor. 9:7–11). Maintenance sowing is giving only our legal tithe but keeping the rest and spending it on ourselves. This guarantees God's supply at the present level only. Abundant sowing is giving well over the legal tenth through having a heart's desire to give in abundance. Multiplication of our resources only comes when we restrict our eating, in other words, deny ourselves, in order to have enough to sow abundantly the following year. God multiplies the seed that we sow, not the seed we eat.

The Bible is very agricultural in its examples and eastern in its culture, thus making the parables Jesus used very applicable in India even today. The farmer is disciplined and sows regularly year by year. A bad year does not deter him. He understands the laws of sowing and reaping. Like a farmer, if you want to prosper financially, you have to take a long-term view. The laws of financial sowing and reaping work relentlessly over years and not just in weeks or months. Sow by faith into good soil, obey the Lord in your giving, water your seed with prayer, and then you will have a harvest.

CHAPTER 12

My Prayer for You to Know the Power of the Cross

This book is intended to help you apprehend the magnitude of what Christ's death on the Cross, burial, and resurrection provided for us. He canceled our debt of sin once and for all so that we might walk in restored relationship with God, free from condemnation.

The Cross provided the power to destroy the old man. We take on a new nature and are liberated out of death into glorious victory. Through the Cross, Christ has given us the power to crucify the flesh and live daily with the strength and life of the Spirit. We can truly find victory and walk in holiness as we live according to the Spirit.

His Cross secured victory over the world and empowers us to enforce the Lordship of Christ everywhere. Christ established an insoluble New Covenant with all humanity, which offers us the beautiful privilege of holy intimacy with our God.

Through the Cross, Jesus Christ forever conquered the curse of sin, sickness, and poverty; He possesses the power to heal and deliver, restore life, provide sufficiency, and grant abundance for every good work.

Our response to all of this provision is simple faith and obedience from a grateful heart. We did nothing to earn the benefits of the Cross; we simply receive by faith. As we conclude, I pray that your eyes have been opened and your heart has responded in faith to all that Christ worked on our behalf through the glorious power of the Cross.

All this has been written to bring the power of the Cross to you. The Holy Spirit wants to make this wonderful covenant a working living reality in your life. Let us be grateful to God for such an incredible and wonderful salvation. Let's thank Him. Let's praise Him. Let's be in awe and wonder of the love of God.

Father, you have shown us wonderful things. We are awed. We are amazed. We are stunned and staggered by the nature of the relationship that You want to have with us. We thought that the blood of Jesus only washed away our sins, taking away our guilt and causing us to escape hell. We had no idea that You wanted to bring us into Your very heart to be intimate with You. We never realized that we should be Your lovers in covenant with You and that You would open up to us the very Holy of Holies. Lord Jesus, You rent the veil of Your flesh and made a holy sanctified way for us to come right into the very heart and center of our God.

Father, we pray we will be those who become possessors of the covenant. We thank You for this unequal covenant. We thank You that there is nothing that we have to do or can do except gratefully receive it. The only response You require from us is to come with a circumcised, obedient heart, and even that is done for us through the grace of baptism. We want to be sanctified lovers of the living God.

Thank You, Jesus. We bless You, Lord. We are so grateful that You are giving us revelation. We are grateful for the Blood that makes it work.

We thank You Father God for Your Holy Spirit who brings the power of Your Grace and the full power of Your Cross into our lives. We thank You! We thank You! We thank You in Jesus's mighty Name! Hallelujah. Amen.

APPENDIX I

My Personal Testimony

For a number of years, after finishing school, I worked as a research scientist for the Kodak Film company in Harrow, England. I was very successful, and it seemed I would have a great future with that company. During those years, I called myself an atheist, having abandoned my childhood Christian upbringing. In 1956–1957, I became interested in the possibility of going to the United States to join the staff of Kodak at their international headquarters in Rochester, New York. I was drawn to the United States of America, where they seemed to appreciate ambitious people like me more readily than they did in England. I thought I could make more money and achieve a more prestigious career in the United States. It was when thinking about these things that, to my surprise, two young Americans arrived at our doorstep. They happened to be Mormon missionaries who were just starting out on their two-year compulsory, post-graduation, door-to-door evangelism program.

I told them that I would be very interested to talk with them about America, but I was not a bit interested in their religion. They had their own agenda and I had mine, so we finally agreed on a compromise. They said that it would take just thirty minutes to teach their Mormon lesson based on the Bible and then afterward they would be happy to talk with me about America for the rest of the evening. So, on that basis, these two missionaries began to visit our home every Monday evening to teach the basic principles of Mormonism.

Thankfully, two things helped me avoid becoming a Mormon. First, I had a solid Christian background through my family, having attended a Baptist Church and Sunday school as a boy for many years. Second, my paternal grandmother had lived her last few years in my parents' home when she was too old to take care of herself. She was a praying, Jesus-loving grandmother who was powerfully filled with the Holy Spirit during the Welsh Revival in 1904. While she lived with us, she became aware of my spiritual condition and decided to target me with her prayers. One day she came to me and said, "Alan, I've been praying for you, and today Jesus spoke to me and said He would save you and call you into ministry and that you would then serve Him for the rest of your life." I thought she was crazy at the time, but I never forgot what she said. A year or two later, she died and went to be with the Lord, but through her prayers of faith, she had already obtained the title deed for my salvation. When the Mormons began to talk to me about the Bible, some scriptures I had learned when I was in Baptist Sunday School began to pop into my mind and contradict what they were saying.

My wife, Eileen, as a girl, had been sent to a Methodist church by her mother. She had loved going to church, and she believed all the right things but lacked a full understanding and commitment. We met at a dance in the hospital where she was working as a nurse. That meeting led to a whirlwind romance, and we were soon married. Once we were married, Eileen stopped going to church because I didn't want to go with her. She was a lover of Jesus, but she had never really met Him or given her life to Him. She believed that He was the Savior of the world, but she had never really experienced His salvation personally. As a teenager, she would go to church several times on a Sunday because she liked the atmosphere and loved the people. However, when she met me, I was disinterested in the things of God, and she had to choose between God and me. She chose me because she did not really know God personally.

We had been married for about five years and lived a happy but totally non-churchgoing life together. Then suddenly everything began to change from the day the Mormons arrived on our doorstep. After one of their early lessons, I borrowed Eileen's old Bible and began to read it. I said to her, "I'm going to prove that these Mormons are not teaching the Bible properly." My purpose was purely an intellectual exercise. I did not intend to get involved with any kind of religion, but I thought, *If these Mormons are going to go around teaching from the Bible, at least they should be accurate about what they teach!* I wasn't hostile to Christians; it didn't do any harm to believe what they believed. It seemed to help some people who needed something to lean on, but it wasn't for me.

Through the provocation of the Mormons, God got hold of me and answered the prayers of my grandmother. At first, I began to read the Bible just to show the inaccuracies of the Mormon teaching. However, as I continued to read, particularly John's Gospel, I began to be gripped by what I was reading concerning the person of Jesus Christ. I began to admire Him in spite of myself and began to wonder if the stories about Him could possibly be true.

Then I began to think, *Suppose these stories are true, and there really was a Jesus just like the Bible describes Him. Suppose there really is a God who created all things and we don't just cease to exist when we die. Suppose there is an afterlife where we live eternally either in hell or with Jesus.* I began to think less and less about the Mormons and more and more about Jesus, and I realized that I had to make a decision about Him.

During this time, and for the first time since becoming an adult, I was introduced to a bold Christian believer. He was certainly the first Christian who ever made an impact on me. He was easily my intellectual equal, which was important to me. He was well educated, highly qualified, and had a very responsible job as the senior engineer of a large nearby city. God had arranged some amazing "coincidences" that brought me into contact with him, and I was prepared to listen to him because I felt he was "my kind" of person.

One evening, Eileen and I went to visit him in his home, and as we sat together, I said to him, "Okay, prove the existence of God to me!" I was ready and prepared with all my best intellectual counterarguments. However, he did not offer any intellectual arguments. Instead, he just told me, in the simplest of terms, about Jesus, how he knew Him personally and loved Him with all his heart. He then explained very briefly the story of the Cross and why Jesus was crucified. He then said to me, "Alan, the reason that God isn't real to you is because of the sin in your life. The only way for you to know God is to allow your sin to be taken away, and the only way for your sin to be taken away is for you to believe that Jesus Christ died on the Cross to pay for your sins. You don't have to understand it, but you do have to decide to believe it, and then you must ask God to forgive your sins on the basis of what Jesus has already done for you."

He came to me with this most simple approach, and it really touched my heart. It certainly was not touching my mind. I had all sorts of philosophical questions, but he went right past those barriers and stuck the sword of God's Word right into my heart. He then went on to say, "If you make a decision to believe in what Jesus has already done for you on the Cross, even though you don't understand it, then the barrier of sin between you and God will be taken away, and you will come to know Him like I do. Alan, Jesus is not dead! He is alive, and if you are willing and you invite Him, He will come by His Spirit into your heart, take over your life, and make a completely new man out of you." Then he said, "Do you want this?"

And to my surprise, I heard myself saying, "Yes." To this day, I still do not know why I said yes, but I guess I was obeying my quickened conscience.

Then he said, "You had better pray."

"How do you pray?"

"Just talk to God the way you have been talking to me."

I got on my knees and prayed an honest prayer. "I am making a decision to believe what Jesus did for me on the Cross even though I don't understand it." I invited Him to come into my heart by His Holy Spirit and take over my life. I didn't just want to join some religion; I really wanted to know Him. I finally said, "If You will truly reveal Yourself to me, then I will give myself to You and will serve You for the rest of my life." It was certainly a wonderful answer to my grandmother's prayers.

Immediately, when I got off my knees, I felt a deep peace within me, and I knew that Jesus had come into my life. That day, I came to know Him and heard His voice speaking in my heart for the first time within hours of that experience. I have continued to live that way for over fifty years. I didn't understand the purpose or the power of the Cross at all at first, but I just decided to believe in it. As the years have gone by, God has continued to teach me, with greater and greater depth, the glory and the power of His wonderful Cross and all that He accomplished through it.

Website: www.cityreachers.net

Other Books by Alan Vincent

Heaven on Earth, Releasing the Power of the Kingdom Through YOU

The Kingdom at War, Using Intercessory Prayer to Dispel the Darkness

The Good Fight of Faith, Following in the Example of Jesus

Invading Babylon, the 7 Mountain Mandate
(Alan Vincent is one of the contributors to this important book.)

Made in the USA
Coppell, TX
04 March 2020